pant
huff
HELP ME!!
huff
PLEASE...
DON'T LET ME DIE IN THIS PLACE!!
SOMEBODY...
HELP!!
AIZAWA'S LOOSE.
I WANT EVERY MAN OUT AFTER HER.
USE ANY MEANS NECESSARY.
SHE MUST BE BROUGHT BACK TO TAO.

EPISODE 1 - I What?!

# WARRIORS OF TAO

## CONTENTS

# WARRIORS OF TAO

Volume 1

By

Shinya Kuwahara

TOKYOPOP®

HAMBURG // LONDON // LOS ANGELES // TOKYO

## *Warriors of Tao Vol. 1*
Created by Shinya Kuwahara

---

Translation - Dan Papia
English Adaptation - Dan Papia
Copy Editors - Alexis Kirsch and Carrisa Knight
Retouch and Lettering - Abelardo Bigting
Production Artists - James Dashiell and Vicente Rivera, Jr.
Cover Design - Anna Kernbaum

Editor - Paul Morrissey
Digital Imaging Manager - Chris Buford
Pre-Press Manager - Antonio DePietro
Production Managers - Jennifer Miller and Mutsumi Miyazaki
Art Director - Matt Alford
Managing Editor - Jill Freshney
VP of Production - Ron Klamert
President and C.O.O. - John Parker
Publisher and C.E.O. - Stuart Levy

A TOKYOPOP® Manga

TOKYOPOP Inc.
5900 Wilshire Blvd. Suite 2000
Los Angeles, CA 90036

E-mail: info@TOKYOPOP.com
Come visit us online at www.TOKYOPOP.com



ISBN: 1-59182-786-8

First TOKYOPOP printing: August 2004

10 9 8 7 6 5 4 3 2 1

Printed in the USA

KARMA HERE.
I'LL CHECK THE SCHOOL.
YOU CHECK HER PARENTS' PLACE.
*ANYWHERE* SHE'S LIKELY TO RUN TO FOR COVER.
FIND AIZAWA AND BRING HER IN. TOP PRIORITY.
GOT IT?

GRAMMAR
HERE I AM, THE STAR OF KENDO CLUB!
TOMA SUGURI REPORTING FOR DUTY!

DIDN'T DO SO HOT ON THAT LAST ENGLISH QUIZ, SO I DROPPED BY DETENTION TO BRUSH UP!!
LET'S ALL HIT THE BOOKS! WHUDDAYA SAY?!
GUESS I'M THE ONLY ONE WHO GOT DETENTION TODAY.
AH, WELL, WHAT THE HECK. YUK-YUK.
AT LEAST I GET OUT OF MY AFTER-SCHOOL CHORES.
WHAT'S UP WITH THAT EVEN THE TEACHER'S NOT HERE.
WHAT A WASTE.
OR MAYBE NOT. I THINK I'LL TAKE A NAP.
I SHOULD DUCK IN HERE AFTER SCHOOL TOMORROW TOO!
pant
pant
HMM?
pant
pant

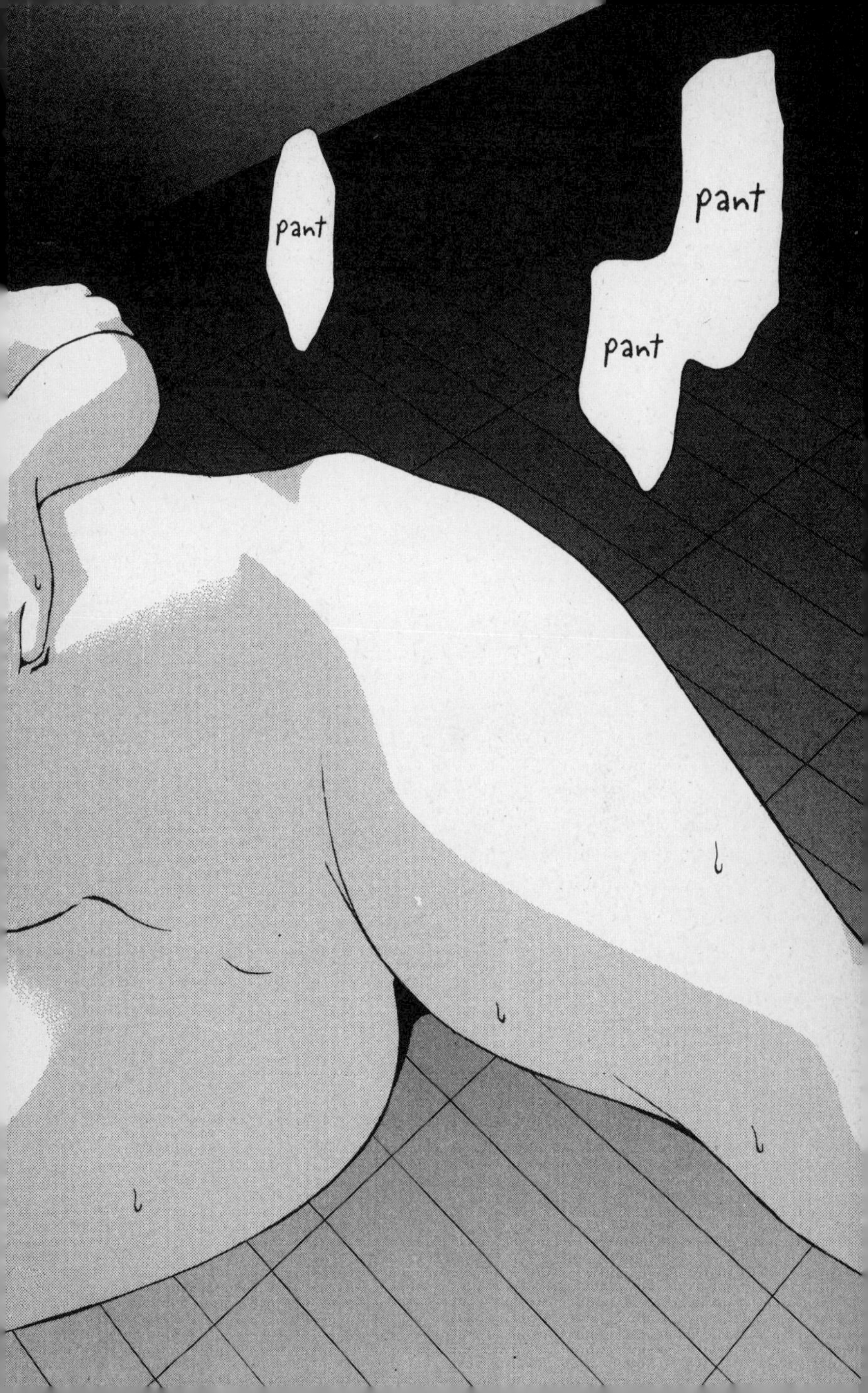
pant
pant
pant

pant

CHECK IT OUT, TOMA!
SOMEONE TOSSED SOME PORNOS IN HERE AGAIN.
HMPH.
IF YOU WANT IT, GO BUY IT. DON'T BE A TRASH PICKER.
rustle
pant
pant
pant
pant

ハア
ハア
ハア
AHH...
YAH!
ACK!
じた
ばた
じた
ばた
......
What's this? A present!?! For me??!
Guess God took pity on my life of homework and flunking quizzes.
Thanks, old man!
I gotta say, this chick is...

...incredibly cute!
I just...

...can't take my eyes off her.
じいいいいっ
HEH-HEH. HI.
HUH?!
NO, WAIT!
Don't do that!
I WASN'T THINKING ANYTHING PERVERTED. IT'S JUST THAT YOU'RE SO...
RIGHT!
CLOTHES! YOU NEED CLOTHES!
HERE! TAKE MINE! YOU CAN WEAR THESE!
HANG ON. I'LL GIVE YOU MY PANTS.
UH... THAT'S OKAY.

HEE-HEE.
Sh- she talked ...!
She talked...
And she laughed!
I'm so so so happy!!
This is better than making a clean cut in kendo!!
Member of the Kendo Club
Oh, baby, you've rocked my world!
ガラッ
WHO'S THAT?!
HEY, NO DUDES ALLOWED! I'M IN THE MIDDLE OF SOMETHING!
Kinda sorta...
I SHOULD POUND YOU!

Wha...??!
He's a foreigner!
K-KARMA...

Shoot, it looks like they know each other.
HUH?
KARMA...?
gulp
His shirt.
YIKES!
His skin.
NO, WAIT.
IT'S NOT WHAT IT LOOKS LIKE! I DIDN'T DO ANYTHING!
YOU SEE, MR. FOREIGNER...
IT'S LIKE...
ENGLISH ...
UM... "PARDON ME"?!
AH...
..."COW ARE YOU?"
Sheesh. No wonder I flunked the quiz.
TOOK A WHILE TO FIND YOU.
WE'VE GOT TO GET BACK TO TAO, MISS ITSUKI AIZAWA.

ブル
ブル
What the hell's a "Tao"?!
HEY, YOU SPEAK JAPANESE, DAMMIT.
More to the point, who is this...
...this girl named Itsuki Aizawa?
Such a lovely name... ♡
MISS ITSUKI AIZAWA.
YOU DON'T WANT TO MAKE ME ANGRY, DO YOU?
.....
GUESS I GOT TO DO THIS.
EVEN THOUGH IT MAY LEAD TO WHAT YOU CALL...
...AN INTERNATIONAL INCIDENT.

BIG DUDE LIKE YOU MAKING THIS POOR LITTLE THING TREMBLE.
THAT'LL TEACH YOU. IN FACT--
HUH--?
グイ
パラ..

But I can take him. We don't have to hide. I can--
Shh!
Quiet!

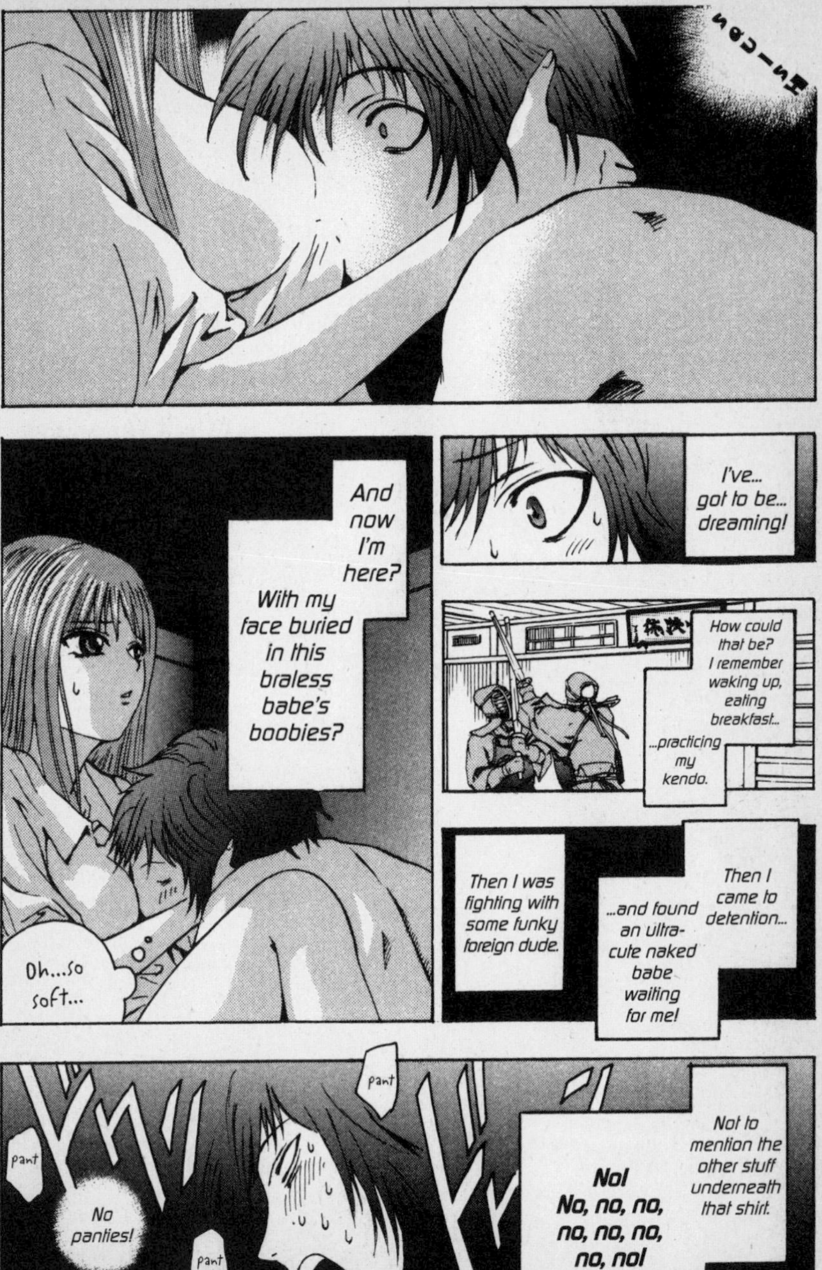
I've... got to be... dreaming!
How could that be? I remember waking up, eating breakfast...
...practicing my kendo.
Then I was fighting with some funky foreign dude.
Then I came to detention...
...and found an ultra-cute naked babe waiting for me!
And now I'm here? With my face buried in this braless babe's boobies?
Oh...so soft...
Not to mention the other stuff underneath that shirt.
No! No, no, no, no, no, no, no, no!
pant
pant
No panties!
pant

Stop!
Derail that train of thought right now! Don't even imagine it!
OH!
Quiet!
Sorry.
THIS IS KARMA.
I'VE SPOTTED AIZAWA. I'VE GOT HER CELL PHONE IN MY HAND. ALL WE HAVE TO DO IS BRING HER IN.
I WANT A MAN AT HER HOME, HER BALLET SCHOOL, *EVERY* COORDINATE.
EVEN MY BALLET SCHOOL...
Can we, like, live here?
Anyway...

...that guy wasn't just some dude.
The way he blocked my special under-the-chin head-butt, he's got something.
And this girl. How did she get in here?
And in the raw, no less?
Aw, well, what's the difference? She's so cute.
I... UH...
...I HAVE A FAVOR TO ASK.
ゴニョ
ゴニョ
WHAT?!
I CAN'T DO THAT!!
PLEASE.
I CAN'T GO HOME. I NEED YOUR HELP.
I...
...NEED...
I NEED YOU...
...TO GO TO THE CHANGING ROOM AND GET MY PANTIES.


* whisper whisper

KENDO CLUB
HEY!
WHERE THE HELL IS THAT TOMA?!
STOMACHACHE. THAT'S WHAT HE SAID AS HE LEFT FOR THE DORMS.
BUT HIS FACE WAS ALL LIKE THIS.
Phys. Ed. Boarding Facility
SO, IT'LL ONLY BE FOR THREE DAYS.
I APPRECIATE IT.
BY THE WAY, MY NAME'S ITSUKI AIZAWA. YEAR TWO, CLASS FOUR.
I APPRECIATE THIS.

D--
DON'T EVEN WORRY ABOUT IT, MISS AIZAWA.
ドキ ドキ ドキ
ドキ ドキッ
WE'RE BOTH STUDENTS. YOU CAN JUST CALL ME ITSUKI.
SURE.
ITSUKI. ♡
NOW THAT YOU MENTION IT, THEY CALL ME--
I KNOW WHAT THEY CALL YOU. YOU'RE THE THIRD BEST KENDO MASTER IN THE COUNTRY.
YOU'RE FAMOUS.
Thank you, kendo!
You see, it's like this. Our school has separate programs for kids going to college and the ones who're just awesome at sports.
The athletic division recruits the best athletes from all over the country. They actively pursue and nurture the best, to say the least.
Everything's separate for the two divisions, all the classes, everything.
So we don't get a lot of babes like Itsuki on our side of the campus.
(We get all the butch chicks. Think gorillas.)
Itsuki's more of an academic type.
Though that doesn't explain why that funky foreigner's after her.

SORRY TO BE SO MUCH TROUBLE.
I JUST NEED A SAFE PLACE TO STAY FOR THREE DAYS, 'TIL AFTER THE AUDITION.
AUDITION?
THAT'S RIGHT.
WHAT THE--?

MODERN BALLET.
I'VE BEEN DOING IT FOR TEN YEARS NOW.
I DON'T KNOW IF I'M ANY GOOD, BUT I THINK I AM.
dribble drool
ARE YOU...
...LOOKING AT ME ALL PERVERTED?
ブル
ブル

WHAT'S THE BIG DEAL?
YOU'VE ALREADY SEEN ALL THERE IS TO SEE.
I... OH...
I-- IT-SUKI?!
NOT TO MENTION...
...YOU HELPED ME OUT OF A JAM. I SHOULD SHOW MY... APPRECIATION.
ダラ
ダラ
ダラ

I THINK YOUR NOSE IS BLEEDING.
はっ
Man, what a crazy fantasy come true.
Only a real sexually frustrated chick's ever gonna go for me.
カァァ
IT'S ALL I HAVE.
BALLET'S MY MOST IMPORTANT THING.
I'M A KLUTZ, THOUGH. I COULD NEVER GET THE STEPS RIGHT. TEACHER'S ALWAYS BAWLING ME OUT.
I TRIED, THOUGH.
ENDLESS PRACTICE.
TEN YEARS.
'TIL FINALLY I BEGAN TO HAVE A LITTLE FAITH IN MYSELF.
SO THIS AUDITION IS REALLY IMPORTANT TO ME.
DON'T WORRY. YOU'LL PASS.

I'LL PROTECT YOU.
JUST FORGET THAT GUY WHO'S AFTER YOU.
HE'S A DORK.
NO, TOMA...
...HE'S NOT.
WHAT?

LISTEN TO ME.
KARMA IS REALLY DANGEROUS. BIG-TIME.
I WANT YOU TO PROMISE ME YOU'LL KEEP AWAY FROM HIM.
Just one look at her face and how can I say no? I feel like I'd do anything she asked.
PLEASE.
I'd do it twice.
One look at those eyes, and it's all over. It's like they suck me in.
クラ..
And the smell of her skin...
Her hair...
I just want to touch it...

サラ…
DON'T!
WHOA!
What did I just...?
I barely touched her.
I'M...
...SO SORRY.
I REALLY DIDN'T MEAN TO...

ITSUKI?
Now she's pissed!

HUH?
WHAT THE HECK?!
IT'S A BLACKOUT!
Yeooww!
Choke!
What just happened?!
NOO!!!
!!
ITSUKI?!

SCUMBAG! HOW'D YOU GET IN HERE?
KLANK
LET GO OF HER! RIGHT NOW!!

You should bow before me, chump.
Come on, you devil warrior you.
SILLY TV DOCTORS.
Rock, paper, scissors, then.
Scissors, paper, go!
Toma?

My...
EEEEEEEEyyyyEEE!!!!
THIS IS WHAT WE CALL POWER, UP ON TAO.

IT'S KNOWN AS A "CODON." SPONTANEOUS BIO-MECHANICAL EVOLUTION.
How did this...? What just happened?!
My eye!
M-MY EYE.
It feels... hot.
"Tao"?! "Codon"?! What's this asshole talking about?
And my eye... Why does it feel...
...like it's on fire?
It's burning!
WELCOME TO FEAR.
PRACTITIONERS OF THE TAO DEAL WITH THIS EVERYDAY.

I CAN'T STAND PEOPLE LIKE YOU.
YOU'RE SO DETERMINED TO HIDE OUT IN SOME SAFE PLACE.
LIVING ONLY FOR YOURSELVES, FORGETTING EVERYTHING ELSE. NO DEVOTION.
AND YOU I ESPECIALLY HATE.
YOU SHOULD DIE.
YOU CHICKEN-SHIT YELLOW MONKEY.
"Devotion"??

* "Hajime No Ippo" is a famous Kodansha manga about boxing.

Ever since I was a little kid, I've buried myself in this kendo world. Kendo, kendo, kendo.
Every stinking day. Thousands of hours of practice.
All just so I could be stronger.
If it can't do that, what's it good for?
I guess I've always known...
...somewhere, in the back of my mind...
...that someday...

...I'd have to protect someone.
I'd meet a girl.
HMPH ...
TOUGH ONE, AREN'T YOU?

Guess that moment has arrived.
This is the girl.
Finally...
...I've found her.

Itsuki and me. That's my future.
ITSUKI !!
HUH?!
I missed? How'd that happen?! It's like I lost my sense of distance!
MONKEY.

Yeeoaaaaaargh!!!
Son...
...of
a...
...bitch!
Life sucks.

I'M NOT DYING YET! FORGET YOU!
BEEP
I GOTTA WATCH OVER ITSUKI!
Hello.
And welcome to Tao.
Your number is 13323433.

Japanese.
Name:
Toma
Suguri.
You've just been registered as a Tao Warrior.
ITSUKIIII!!
ITSUKI!!!
Your Tao powers will begin their transfer when you hear the tone.
ITSU--
HUH?!

WHAT THE...
...HELL?

WHAT THE FUCK IS THIS PLACE??!
YEAAAAAGGH!!!

The Tao is a separate world unto itself, founded on the highest principles
A host world for all those endowed with the calling, all those compelled to fight.

WHAT THE--?!
WELCOME TO TAO.
THIS IS QUITE INCREDIBLE, MR. TOMA.
YOU'RE THE FIRST GUEST WE'VE EVER HAD ARRIVE ENTIRELY OF HIS OWN FREE WILL.

YOU SEE, YOUR CHANCES OF BEING CHOSEN ARE SO SMALL TO BEGIN WITH...
APART FROM YOU, THERE ARE FIVE OTHER EARTHLINGS. THE ODDS OF ANY GIVEN CANDIDATE BEING SELECTED IS, BASICALLY, SIX BILLION TO ONE.
HAVE TO ADMIRE HUMAN DETERMINATION.
......
OH.
YOUR RIGHT EYE. THAT'S YOUR TAO ISSUE PATCH.
I WOULDN'T TOUCH IT JUST YET. YOUR FACE NEEDS TIME TO HEAL.
HOLY SHIT...
WHERE IN THE WORLD AM I??!
WE JUST TOLD YOU. YOU'RE ON TAO.
I THINK THIS ONE MIGHT BE A LITTLE SLOW. ♡

AND WHO ARE YOU TWO SUPPOSED TO BE?!
THOSE GOOFY COSTUMES. WHAT IS THIS? HALLOWEEN?!
YOU'RE HERE TO FIGHT.
ON BEHALF OF ALL HUMAN-KIND.
?!
ALL HUMAN-KIND ??!
FIGHT WHO ?!
YOU'RE A WARRIOR OF TAO.
?!
!?
THERE ARE SIX AT PRESENT, INCLUDING YOU.
THE OTHER FIVE WILL BE BACK SHORTLY.
!?
I JUST REMEMBERED, ITSUKI!
THERE'S THIS GIRL, ITSUKI AIZAWA!
THAT'S RIGHT.
SHE'S ONE OF EARTH'S WARRIORS, TOO.
A VERY CHARMING ONE. THERE IS POWER IN HER INNOCENCE.
YOU SEE, THE SELECTION PROCESS IS RANDOM. WARRIORS ARE PICKED FROM A POOL OF ABLE MEN AND WOMEN BETWEEN 15 AND 40 YEARS OLD.
SORT OF LIKE A LOTTERY. ♡

End of EPISODE 1 - I What?!

# WARRIORS OF TAO

IT'S QUITE SIMPLE, MR. TOMA...
...YOUR INTENT WAS SO STRONG, THAT YOU *WILLED YOURSELF* TO TAO. AND NOW YOU SHALL CHAMPION ALL OF HUMANKIND. ♡
*I WHAT ?!*

I MEAN --!
WHAT'S WITH YOU, TOMA?
MOPING OVER YOUR BREAKFAST LIKE YOU'RE IN SOME TRANCE?
YOU DON'T LIKE IT?
I WHAT ??
Good morning.
I'm back at the cafeteria.
Shoot, practice is starting.
This is crazy!
Just a second ago I was on Tao--whatever that is.
I was talking to these two weirdo twins. Something about how all mankind needed saving and how I'd just volunteered!!

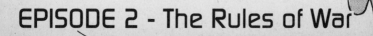

# EPISODE 2 - The Rules of War

chomp
chomp
chomp
DAMMIT, SAITO! WHAT DO YOU THINK YOU'RE DOING?!
THAT WAS MY PIECE OF WIENER-SHAPED SQUID YOU JUST ATE.
CREEP!!
HEY, YOU SNOOZE, YOU LOSE.
SPIT IT OUT!
......
Stupid Saito...
The wiener-shaped squid that the dorm lady makes.
That's my usual breakfast.
poink tap poink
HEY.
YOU KNOW YOU'RE BLEEDING?
That must mean...
WHAT THE HECK?
IT WAS ALL A DREAM!
......
And even my eye. Right back where it was.

Kendo Club Dojo
YAAHHHHHH!
It felt like such a real dream.
That freaky foreigner with that distinctive face.
And how my eye felt like it was on fire. I can **still** feel it.
I dreamt that?
Or...
...could it be...?
HEY! TOMA!
WHERE DO YOU THINK YOU'RE GOING?!
2年4組

* Second Year, Class Four

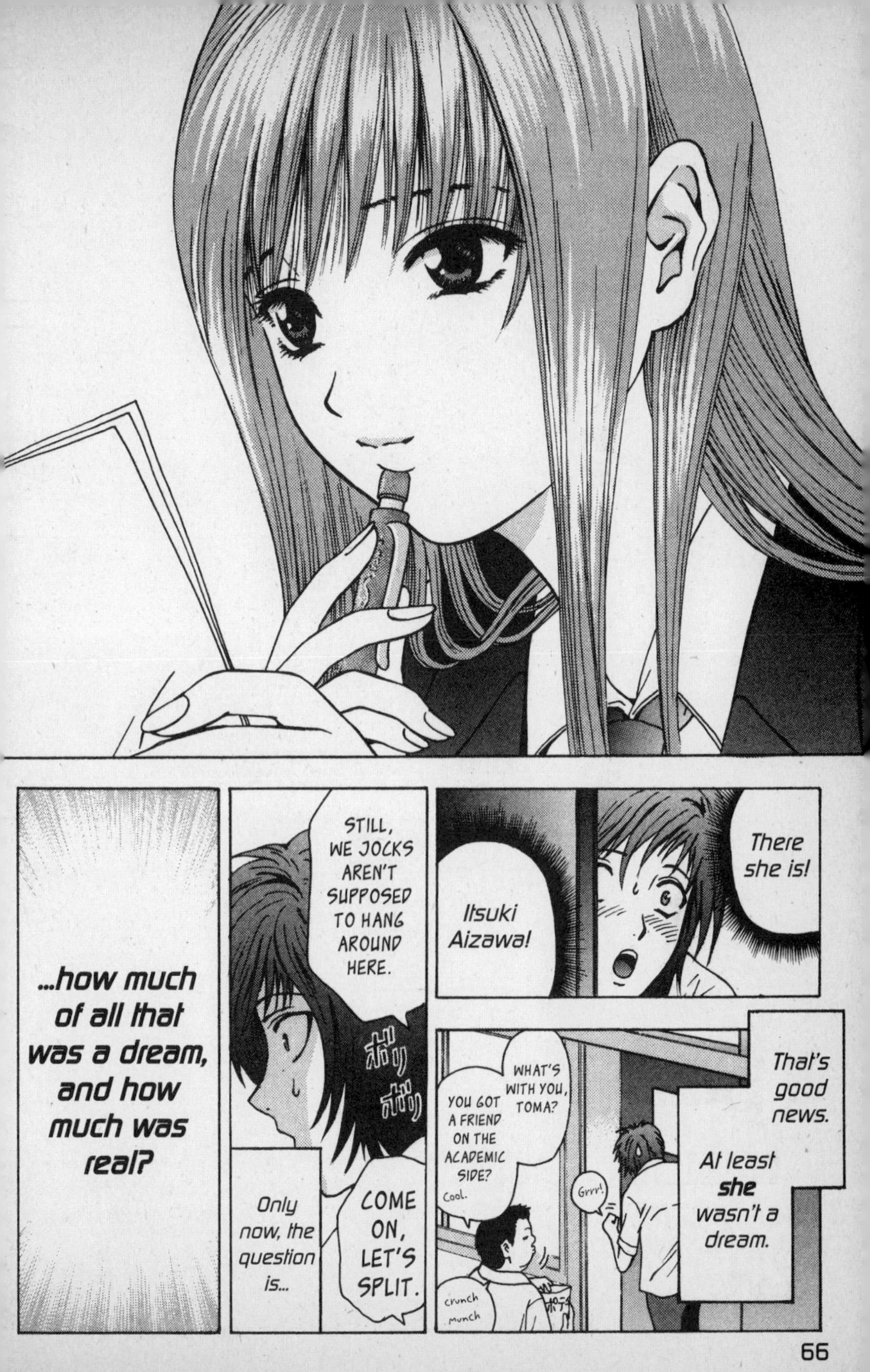
There she is!
Itsuki Aizawa!
That's good news.
At least she wasn't a dream.
WHAT'S WITH YOU, TOMA?
YOU GOT A FRIEND ON THE ACADEMIC SIDE?
Cool.
Grrr!
crunch munch
STILL, WE JOCKS AREN'T SUPPOSED TO HANG AROUND HERE.
COME ON, LET'S SPLIT.
Only now, the question is...
...how much of all that was a dream, and how much was real?

For one thing, did I really see her naked?
Does that funky foreign dude really exist?
Now I'm totally confused. Except...
...she's **still** the sexiest thing ever. That's for sure.
Munch
Crunch
ポテトがうまい
チップス
WILL YOU SHUT UP WITH ALL THAT CRUNCHING?!
HAVEN'T YOU EATEN ENOUGH FOR TODAY?!

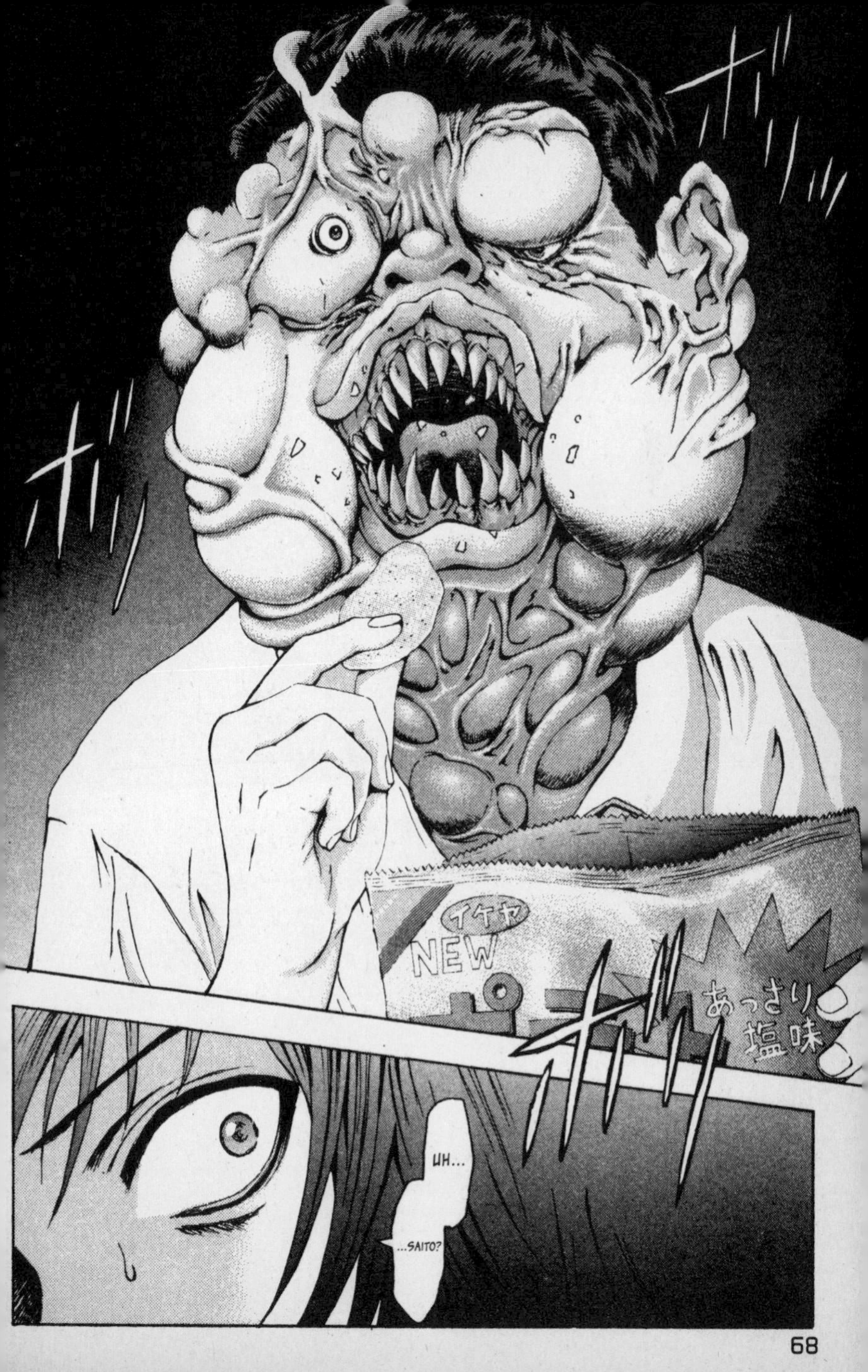
イケヤ
NEW
あっさり塩味
UH...
...SAITO?

I know.
I don't know **what** it is.
I just keep feeling hungry.
Like I got to eat, can't stop. It's weird.
It's like...
...I don't feel right. I--!
Hey!
Toma? Why are you looking at me like that?
What is it?
Something on my face?
YEAH, VIERI'S THE BEST PLAYER IN THAT "WEDDING ELEVEN" GAME...
Urp.
HUH?
EEK.
WHO?
HOW?
Aggg...!

Weeeaarghh!
Splah hah wah!
HEY...
...GUYS?
NOOOO!
STOP!!
QUIT IT!!!
gasp

That sounded like...
...Itsuki's scream.
ITSUKI!!

NOOOOO!!...!!
AIZAWA!!!

Attention! All residents of this planet!!
We are Evolved Beings.
We represent a united force, a confed-eracy of worlds...
...formed to protect life and the universe, to regulate and manage, by any means necessary.
UGGAA!!
UHOOOOOGH!

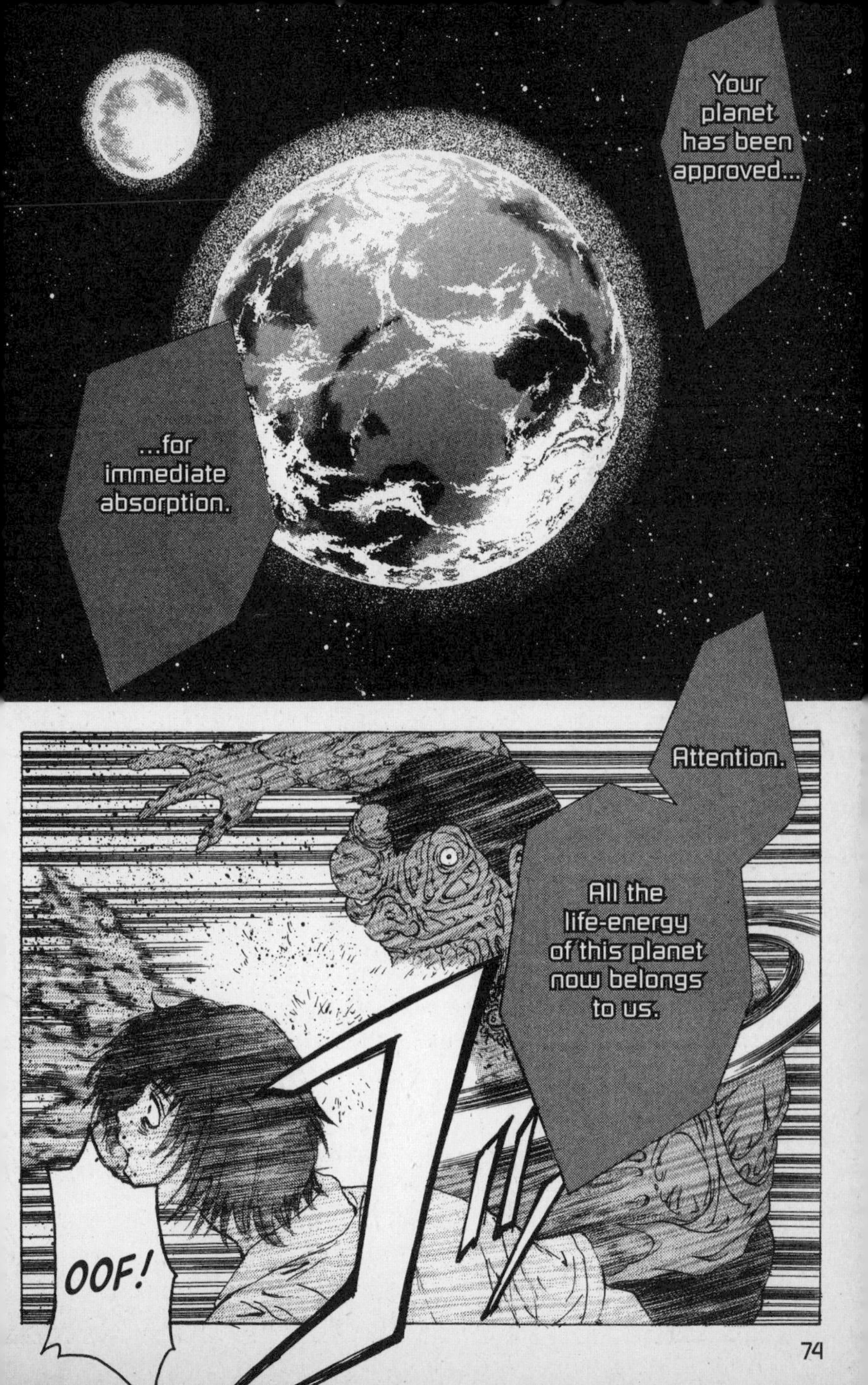
Your planet has been approved...
...for immediate absorption.
Attention.
All the life-energy of this planet now belongs to us.
OOF!

Aaggg!
NOOOO!!
MMPH!
HELP!
I...
ITSUKI...
Heh!
Har!
MMFFPH!
YOU!
WHAT DO YOU THINK...
...YOU'RE DOING TO MY ITSUK--?

ITS--!
ITSUKIIII!!
30% of you have been designated as "feeders."
The rest of you are "food."

For the "feeders"...
...the power of rapid evolution will be transmitted to them via DNA staining.
All other physical life forms will give to the galactic cause by being eaten and allowing Feeders to absorb their energy.
Upon feeding completion, uneaten individuals designated as "food" will be transformed for optimal energy absorption.
This energy will be recoverable at a later date.
Aaagggghrr!
swuck
Pwink
Pwoonk
slikt
Heh.
Wheh.
STOP!
YOU STOP THAT!

Glub blub glub blub blub!
OH...
... GOD ...
ITSUKI...
Understand, Earthlings.
You are not dying in vain.

We too are life-forms, born of the same universe.
And like you, we have made great and noble sacrifices...
...for the propagation of ourselves and the continued survival of select other life-forms, as well. This is our charge.
We repeat.
You will most certainly not have died in vain.
ITSUKIIIII!!

ITSU...
...
SHLOOP
NOOOOO!!!
IT-SUKIII!!

HUH?
IT MAY INTEREST YOU TO KNOW, THE IMAGES YOU'VE JUST SEEN ARE *NOT* FICTIONAL.
THEY ARE PICTURES OF A GRAVE SITUATION.
ONE THAT WILL SOON CONFRONT PLANET EARTH.
AAARRRGGGHHH!!!
ITSUKI!!! THOSE MONSTERS ARE EATING HER!
IMAGES! YOU WERE JUST LOOKING AT MOVING IMAGES, YOU *MORON!*
ITSUKI AIZAWA IS STILL OKAY!
LIKE... ...IN THE MOVIES?
SHE'S ALL RIGHT?
NOT LIKE IN MOVIES! PICTURES OF THE *FUTURE!* THIS IS WHAT'S *GOING* TO HAPPEN!
I TOLD YOU--HE *IS* SLOW. ♡
I GET IT. I GET IT.
NO MONSTERS ATE ITSUKI, RIGHT?
THAT'S A RELIEF.

BUT... UH...
...YOU MEAN SHE'S GOING TO BE EATEN?
Grrrr...
COULD YOU PLEASE TRY TO KEEP UP?
ギリ
ギリ
NOW, NOW. ♡
So, that flick...
...showed stuff that could really happen.
PRECISELY. ♡
VERY GOOD.
WHEW...
GLAD SHE'S STILL ALIVE.
THE SACRIFICIAL PLANET IS JUST ABOUT TO BE DETERMINED.
THAT'S WHAT YOU'RE HERE FOR.
TO FIGHT ON BEHALF OF EARTH IN THE INTERPLANETARY TOURNAMENT.

ONLY ONE PLANET CAN SURVIVE ACCORDING TO THE PLAN.
ONLY ONE.
FOR THE SAKE OF THE PRESERVATION OF LIFE, ALL WORLDS WILL TAKE PART.
AND ALL BECOME SACRIFICES...
...TO THE SURVIVING PLANET.
IN THIS UNIVERSE, THERE ARE 87 INTELLI-GENT AND EVOLVED WORLDS.
IF SOME MEASURE IS NOT TAKEN FOR THE SELECTION OF SURVIVORS AND FERTILIZERS, IF YOU WILL, THE LIFE-FORCE WILL NOT SURVIVE.
COHABITATION OF THE UNIVERSE WILL NO LONGER WORK, YOU SEE.
IN ORDER FOR LIFE TO CONTINUE ...
...THE BEINGS OF ONE WORLD MUST EVENTUALLY FEED ON THE FLESH AND BLOOD OF ANOTHER.

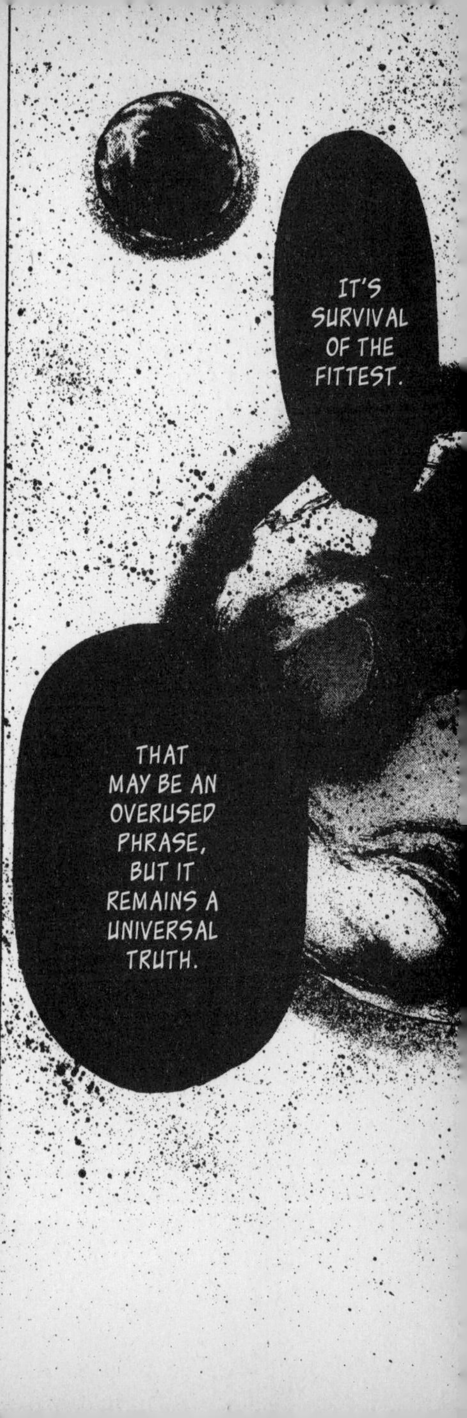
IT'S SURVIVAL OF THE FITTEST.
THAT MAY BE AN OVERUSED PHRASE, BUT IT REMAINS A UNIVERSAL TRUTH.

FROM THE ANCIENT DAYS ...
...GALACTIC WARS HAVE BEEN THE SUREST WAY OF DETERMINING WHO SURVIVES AND WHO DIES.
What the hell are they talking about?
This whole speech is totally over my head.
OF COURSE, NONE WOULD BE FOOLISH ENOUGH TO ATTACK ANOTHER LIFE-FORM TO SUCH AN EXTREME THAT IT COMPLETELY PERISHES.
I don't get any of this, but whatever it is...
...that can't...
...really be the future.
It's a gag.
It has to be.
CLENCH

IN THAT INSTANCE, THE OVERRIDING CONCEPT IS INTERVENTION.
A CONFEDERACY FORMED TO KEEP PEACE AND ORDER IS DELEGATED BY ALL THE PLANETS.
THAT CONFEDERACY IS KNOWN AS THE "TAO."
ITS RULES ARE DETERMINED BY THE VICTORS OF THE TOURNAMENT.
THE "TAO" OVERSEES THE UNIVERSAL COMPETITION ...
...IN WHICH THE PLAYERS STAKE THEIR FUTURE ON THE GAME.
NOT UNLIKE JOUSTS OR DUELS IN YOUR OLD-FASHIONED COLISEUMS.
AND YOU HAVE BEEN CHOSEN TO REPRESENT EARTH.
NUTS.
YOU ARE A GLADIATOR ON BEHALF OF EARTH, SIR TOMA SUGURI.
TOTALLY NUTS.

YOU REALLY THINK WE CAN USE THIS MONKEY?
!!
YOU...
...YOU SCUM BUZZARD...
!!
Oh, Itsuki...you smell so sweet.

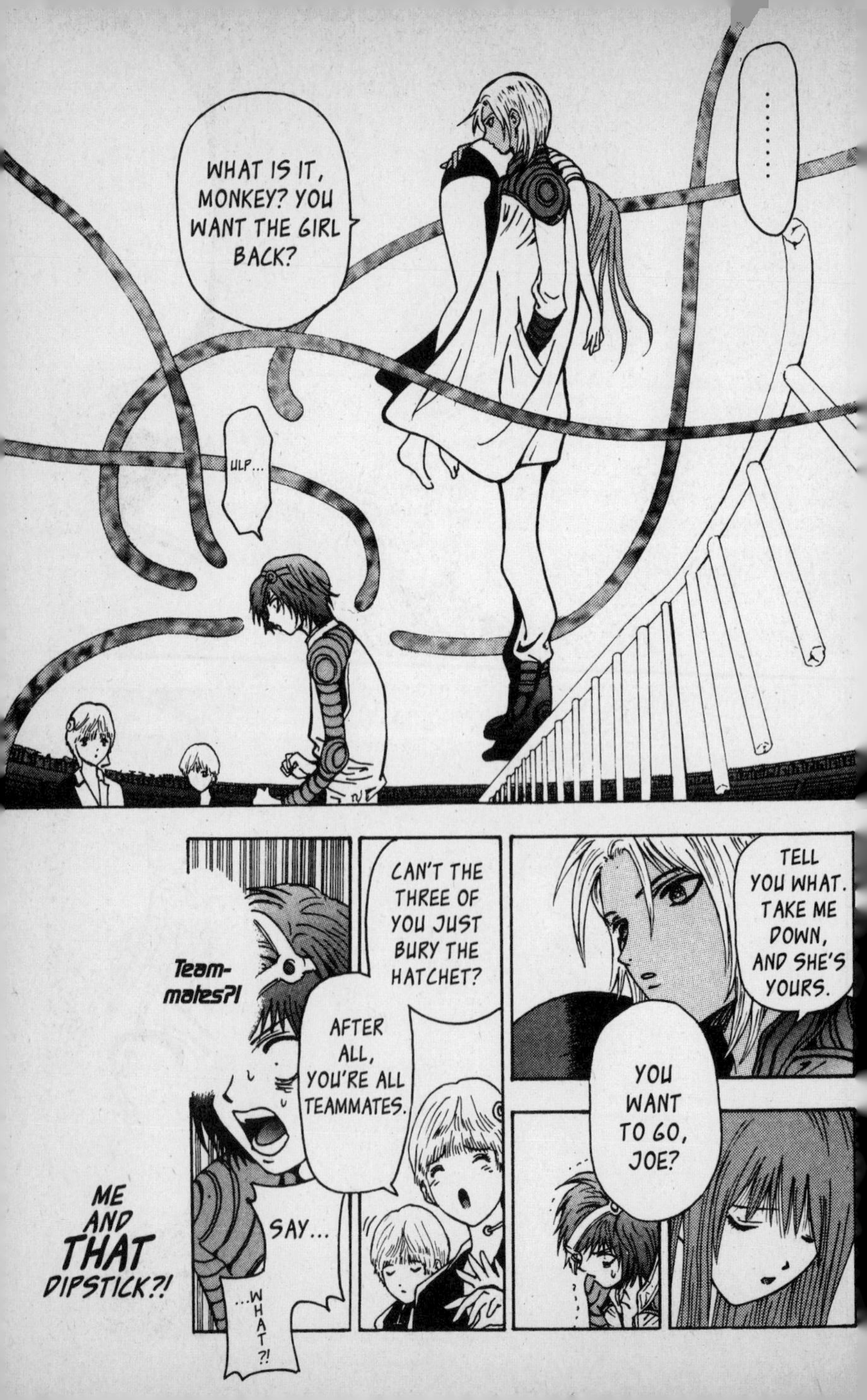
......
WHAT IS IT, MONKEY? YOU WANT THE GIRL BACK?
ULP...
TELL YOU WHAT. TAKE ME DOWN, AND SHE'S YOURS.
YOU WANT TO GO, JOE?
CAN'T THE THREE OF YOU JUST BURY THE HATCHET?
AFTER ALL, YOU'RE ALL TEAMMATES.
SAY...
...WHAT?!
Team-mates?!
ME AND THAT DIPSTICK?!

IT'S LIKE SHE SAID.
WE'VE GOT SIX GLADIATORS HERE, AND I'M THE TEAM LEADER.
YOU'RE MY RESPONSI-BILITY.
I'VE GOT TO MAKE SURE WE'RE ALL UP TO SNUFF.
I'd like to snuff him.
AFTER ALL, IF ONE OF THOSE OTHER TEAMS TAKES US DOWN...
...OUR WHOLE PLANET'S LUNCH.
Dude, talk about pressure.
He seems different from the last time we met.
He was just sizing me up then.
THIS IS TOO MUCH FOR A MONKEY LIKE YOU.
I can't...
...I can't beat this guy.

HOWEVER ...
AIZAWA HERE COULD BE USEFUL TO ME.
IF SHE COMPLETES HER TRAINING, SHE COULD BE A REAL FORCE.
I KNOW THIS--SHE CAN BE A SOLDIER I CAN USE.
"Use"?!
"Soldier"?!
MODERN BALLET.
I DON'T KNOW IF I'M ANY GOOD, BUT I THINK I AM.
You bastard!!!
You leave her alone!!

BUT YOU, I DON'T THINK YOU'LL DO MUCH FOR ME.
I THINK FOR THE GOOD OF YOUR PLANET...
...YOU SHOULD JUST DIE RIGHT NOW.
......
MR. TOMA HAS BEEN SENT BACK TO HIS OWN WORLD.
WE'D LIKE TO REMIND YOU THAT MURDERING A FELLOW TEAMMATE IS AGAINST THE RULES, KARMA.
JUDGES CAN'T BE EXPECTED TO OVERLOOK SOMETHING LIKE THAT.
YOUR INTENTIONS ARE CLEAR.
GET RID OF TOMA, OPEN A PLACE ON YOUR TEAM.
....

YOU'D LIKE TO KEEP DOING THAT UNTIL THE TEAM MEETS WITH YOUR SATISFACTION.
AND FIND A REPLACEMENT THAT'S MORE TO YOUR LIKING.
UNFORTUNATELY, IF WE WERE TO ALLOW THAT, WE'D BE GIVING YOU AN UNFAIR ADVANTAGE. THAT WOULD MAKE THE WHOLE LOTTERY PROCESS MEANINGLESS.
HMPH.
OF COURSE...
...IF ONE OF MY CONTENDERS WERE TO HAVE A FATAL ACCIDENT IN THE COURSE OF TRAINING...
*THAT* WOULD BE PERFECTLY LEGAL.
......
YOU MAY INTEND TO KILL MR. TOMA ON THE PRACTICE GROUNDS.
WHAT A SHAME. I THOUGHT IT SO CUTE THE WAY HE ACTED SO SLOW.
WHAT ACT? HE'S A DOPE.
OH WELL. ♡
BY THE WAY, WE NEVER GOT A CHANCE TO EXPLAIN THE RULES OF ATOMIZATION TO TOMA.
HE DOESN'T REALIZE THAT HE MAY LOSE HIS BIO-MECHANICAL ATTACHMENTS WHEN HE RE-MATERIALIZES. ♡
I DO HOPE HE ISN'T HEADED ANYWHERE TOO PUBLIC...

WILL YOU LOOK AT THE GUY?
YUCK. IS HE FOR REAL?
HEY, I KNOW HIM. HE'S FROM THE KENDO TEAM.
YEAH, THAT'S TOMA SUGURI.
THAT IS TOTALLY DEPRAVED.
IS THAT WHY THEY CALL THEM "BLOW FISH?"
I ALWAYS SAID, TOMA'S A MAN'S MAN.
Practice, get strong.
And knock that freaking foreigner's block off.
I've got to get Itsuki Aizawa back!!
That's what I've got to do.
Ah, Itsuki.
That's nice.
Ow.
Not so hard... oh...oh... ♡
Oh yeah. ♡
End of EPISODE 2 - The Rules of War

# WARRIORS OF TAO

# Heroic Youth from White Cloud High Courts Carp

ıite Cloud High School's Toma Suguri, a national Kendo champion ranking third in the country, gave new meaning to e term "cod piece" yesterday when he was found just after 8:30 a.m. naked in the school pond with a fish attached to his ɔre-personal components. The fish with which Toma was intimately liaisoned was reportedly a prized carp belonging to e school director and valued at several million yen. Toma was discovered when several students heard "splashing and ɔaning" and came to investigate. Toma had apparently fallen asleep, relaxed perhaps by the pleasurable sensations of s communing with nature. Upon awakening, Toma was heard to say, "You bastard! You leave her alone!" It is still unclear to what he meant. This picture was taken just as he was regaining consciousness...

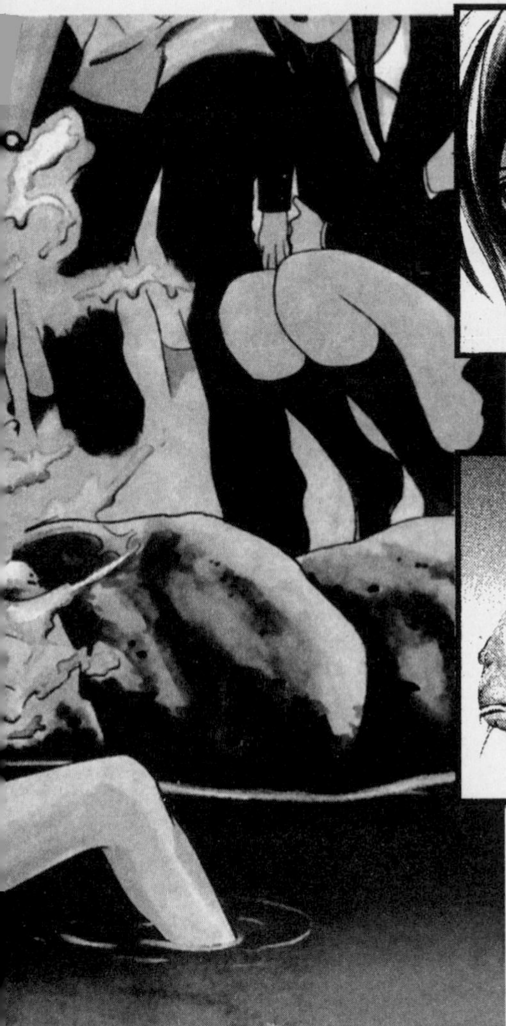

★ *Toma had a number of fans on campus prior to the incident.*

★ *This prized colored carp was also popular with the students.*

Super Cool School News and Reviews
Swords and Sports
This Sucks!!
Intercollegiate
Kendo Champ
has Feel for Fi
Innocence Lost at 17

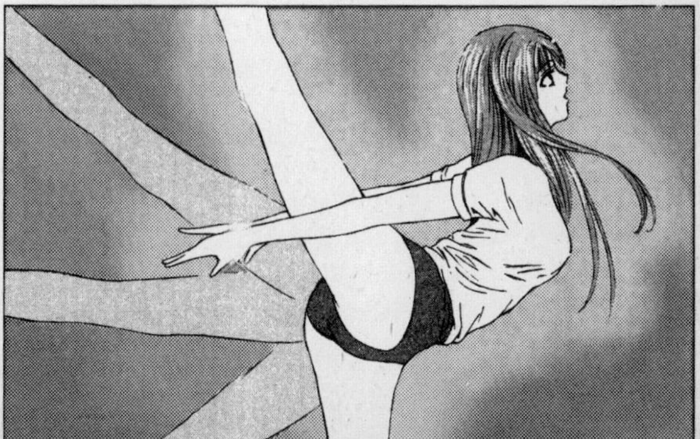

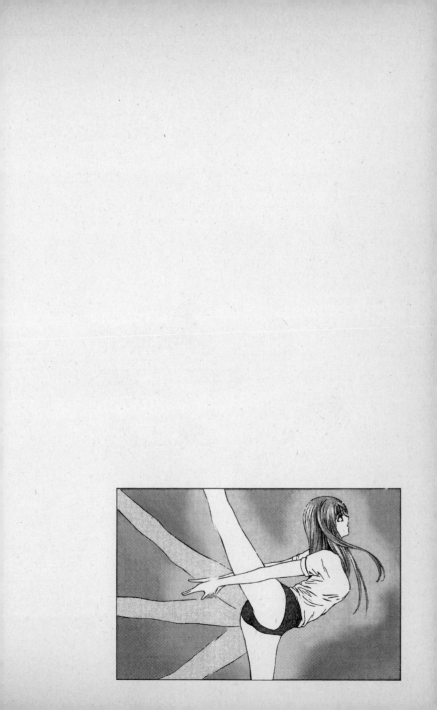

"HEROIC YOUTH COURTS CARP..."
"WHITE CLOUD HIGH SCHOOL'S TOMA SUGURI, A NATIONAL KENDO CHAMPION RANKING THIRD IN THE COUNTRY, GAVE NEW MEANING TO THE TERM "COD PIECE" YESTERDAY WHEN HE WAS FOUND JUST AFTER 8:30 A.M. NAKED IN THE SCHOOL POND WITH A FISH ATTACHED TO HIS MORE PERSONAL COMPONENTS..."
.....
"TOMA WAS DISCOVERED WHEN SEVERAL STUDENTS HEARD 'SPLASHING AND MOANING' AND CAME TO INVESTIGATE..."
"TOMA HAD APPARENTLY FALLEN ASLEEP, RELAXED PERHAPS BY THE PLEASURABLE SENSATIONS OF HIS COMMUNING WITH NATURE."
Nurse's Office
"UPON AWAKENING, TOMA WAS HEARD TO SAY, 'YOU BASTARD! YOU LEAVE HER ALONE!' IT IS STILL UNCLEAR AS TO WHAT HE MEANT."
ブル
ブル

## EPISODE 3 - Enter: The Hardcore Wanderer

[redacted]

DO YOU HAVE ANY IDEA OF THE FLACK I HAD TO TAKE FROM THE PRINCIPAL JUST BECAUSE OF YESTERDAY?
THEY ACCUSED ME OF NOT DOING MY JOB! "THIS IS WHAT HAPPENS WHEN YOU SEND A GIRL TO DO A MAN'S JOB."
EVEN CALLED ME A TEMPTRESS. I HAD TO STAND THERE WHILE HE LEERED AND GUFFAWED FOR THREE WHOLE HOURS.
Kyoko Himekawa
Physical Education Liaison
OR PERHAPS THE PROBLEM IS...
...THOSE ENORMOUS BREASTS OF YOURS.
YUK YUK YUK.
AFTER ALL... THEY'RE LARGER THAN THE OTHER TEACHERS', AND BOYS ARE IMPRESSIONABLE.
HEY, TOMA!
ARE YOU LISTENING TO ME?!
THE FIRST THING I NEED IS FOR YOU TO TELL ME EXACTLY WHAT HAPPENED!

I...
MAYBE IT'S TRUE.
THE BOY'S JUST SEXUALLY FRUSTRATED.
I SUPPOSE IT MAKES SENSE.
AT THAT AGE.
PRACTICING ALL THE TIME, NO ROOM FOR GIRLFRIENDS.
ADMITTED WITH SO MUCH CEREMONY. SO MANY HIGH HOPES FOR HIM EVERY DAY.
I IMAGINE HE MUST HAVE A LOT OF STRESS.
?
I GUESS IT'S MY DUTY AS PHYSICAL EDUCATION LIAISON TO DO WHAT I CAN TO RELIEVE HIM.
YOU KNOW, TOMA...
...I THINK IT MIGHT BE BEST...
...IF YOU JUST CAME OUT AND TOLD ME ABOUT THE FEELINGS YOU'RE HAVING.

IF YOU WANT TO KNOW HOW I FEEL, YOU SHOULD READ EPISODES ONE AND TWO.
IF YOU STILL DON'T UNDERSTAND, BUY ANOTHER COPY.
HUH?
IN FACT, WHY NOT READ ALL SIX VOLUMES OF KUWAHARA'S UCHIKOSHI-KUN? GOOD MANGA!
HUH?
ANYWAY.
I GOT TO GO TO PRACTICE.
BUT, TOMA! WAIT!
YOU STILL HAVEN'T TOLD ME WHAT'S FRUSTRATING YOU!
AND YOU NEED TO REST, YOUNG MAN.
A FISH BITE CAN TAKE MORE OUT OF YOU THAN YOU THINK!
MR. TOMA!
I'm sorry, Miss Himekawa.
I appreciate your concern.
But I don't think you'd believe what's troubling me.
Saving the world.
The sacrificial planet and all that.

TO TELL THE TRUTH...
...I DON'T EVEN THINK I BELIEVE IT.
SOME KIND OF JOUSTING TOURNAMENT BETWEEN PLANETS TO DECIDE WHO GETS TO SURVIVE.
SIX GLADIATORS CHOSEN OUT OF SIX BILLION PEOPLE TO DEFEND THE EARTH.
AND THOSE DOPEY TWINS WITH THEIR BUTT-HUGGING HOT PANTS!!
....
But...
...I do believe I met a girl named Itsuki.
And I feel like I really have been to Tao.
RIGHT HERE IN MY EYE.
HERE'S THE PROOF.

THIS...
...THIS IS NOT MY EYE!
IT'S SOME KIND OF FALSIE!
THOSE CREEPS!
WHAT THE HELL DID THEY DO TO ME?
YESTERDAY...
...THE WHOLE THING SHOOK ME UP SO MUCH...
IT WAS ENOUGH OF A SHOCK TO CONVINCE ME I WASN'T DREAMING.
AND IF THIS WHOLE THING'S REAL...
...WELL, THEN, I ONLY HAVE ONE CHOICE.

I'VE GOT TO FIND A FUNKY FOREIGNER NAMED KARMA AND KNOCK HIM ON HIS ASS!
I'VE GOT TO GET MY ITSUKI AIZAWA BACK!
WHOA, LOOK!
TOMA'S AT IT AGAIN! BLOOD EVERYWHERE.
GUESS HE'S TRYING TO KILL HIMSELF BECAUSE OF THAT ARTICLE.
WELL, SNAP A PIC, QUICK. WE CAN SELL THIS ONE TO THE NATIONAL PRESS!!
Got to practice!
GRRRRR!!!
Got to get stronger!

Stronger! Stronger than Karma...!
HAI-YAH!
YEE-OW!
PARRY!
ATTACK!
SWING!
crack
SMACK
BRUTAL BLOW!
Stronger than stone!
CRAP!
ORDINARY PRACTICE ISN'T GOING TO GET ME THERE!
LET'S SEE. WHAT OTHER KINDS OF STRENGTH ARE THERE?
WHAT ARE YOU DOING, TOMA?! READING MANGA IN THE DOJO!!
PLUS THOSE ARE MY MANGA!
GET BACK HERE!
....
POOR TOMA.
HE CAN'T WORK OFF HIS SEXUAL FRUSTRATION THROUGH SPORTS ALONE.
It's all too obvious.

OKAY! I'M JUST LIKE BRUCE LEE IN "ENTER THE DRAGON"!
I'M THIS GENERATION'S MARTIAL ARTS MASTER!
I HAVE ARMS OF STEEL!
JUST LIKE GTO!
Arm-wrestling a hundred dudes like Onizuka!
POOR BOY. HIS BASER DESIRES ARE LEADING HIM TO VIOLENCE.
THIS IS NO GOOD. I'M GOING TO HAVE TO DO SOMETHING.
AND I SHOULD SHOW THOSE IDIOTS IN "INITIAL D" HOW TO REALLY DRIVE!
VROOM
ZOOM
HE'S GIVING IN TO HIS HORMONE-DRIVEN RAGE, JUST AS I FEARED.
Raaaarrrrrh!
WHA?

NOW A LITTLE FIELD PRACTICE!
OW!
WHO IS THIS GUY??!
EAT THIS, STREET PUNK!
TAKE THAT, BIKER GEEKS!
HEY!
STINKING BOOK WORMS!
Taste some foot, you manga nerds!
COME ON!
ALL OF YOU! LET'S GO!
OH NO !!!
TWO DAYS LATER ...
THIS COULD GET VERY UGLY!

...BIT OFF MORE THAN YOU COULD CHEW, SCUMBAG.
YOU HEAR?
ARR!
YOU'RE GONNA DIE!
GONNA GET KILLED!
YIKES!
OH NO!!
LOOK!
LOOK HOW MANY THERE ARE!

I'LL TEAR YOU APART!
GROWL !!
COME ON, RUSH AT ME. I DARE YOU! ♡
P-POLICE!!
GOT TO CALL THEM BEFORE TOMA GETS SQUASHED TO DEATH!
!!

WHAT ...?
WHAT'S WITH YOU, YOU DUMBASS?!
THIS TIME WE'RE DONE GOOFING AROUND!
YOU STILL WANT TO GO?!

Shut up!!
YOU CHUMPS ARE GOOFS ALL THE WAY! HOW AM I SUPPOSED TO BEAT KARMA IF I CAN'T EVEN SPAR WITH YOU?!
SO, YEAH, I STILL WANT TO GO! NO CHOICE!
SEE!
Next time, I drop Karma on his ass!
No more screw-ups!
Got to practice, get stronger!
Stronger than Karma, take him down!
And get Itsuki back!
And then... when she's back...
OH...
...THANK YOU, TOMA.

OH, TOMA. OH, SWEET TOMA.
NOW, NOW, GIRL.
Karma
OH, TOMA.
HA HA... YOU'RE CUTE, YOU KNOW THAT?
HERE, I WANT TO REALLY THANK YOU.
YOU DON'T MIND, DO YOU?
THAT'LL BE SOOOO NICE. ♥
HEH HEH HEH! HA HA.
HE'S NUTS.
THE DUDE'S BLOWN A FUSE.
IT'S MAKING ME SICK.
WAY TOO MUCH JUICE IN HIM.
FOR REAL!
HE'S ALREADY KNOCKED OUT TEN OF OUR GUYS!

THIS IS AN EMBARRASSMENT!
SOMEONE BETTER HURRY UP AND CRACK HIS SKULL!
OR ELSE I'M GONNA BE TOO ASHAMED TO WALK THE STREETS!
YO!
GIVE HIM A SQUIRT.
JUST WAIT, ITSUKI!! I'M COMING!
HUH?
ACK--
WAH-HA-HA! TAKE THAT, MO-RON!
LET'S SEE HOW YOU FIGHT BLIND-FOLDED!
N-not good.
It went all the way in!
And it hurts!
GEE, WHAT'S THE MATTER?
SOMETHING IN YOUR EYE?

SERVES YOU RIGHT...
...PUKE!
Crapola.
I couldn't shut my eyes fast enough!!
Now what?!
FRIGGIN' PRETTY BOY!
YOU TICK ME OFF, YOU KNOW THAT?!
DON'T YOU KNOW WHEN TO QUIT?!
Itsukiii!!!
YOU'RE MESSING WITH THE BIG BOYS NOW!
I gotta save Itsuki!! Don't they get it?!
OOF!
NOW YOU'RE REALLY DEAD!!
H-HEY, DUDE! THAT'S GOING TOO FAR!
YO! COOL OFF!
YOU BAS-TID!

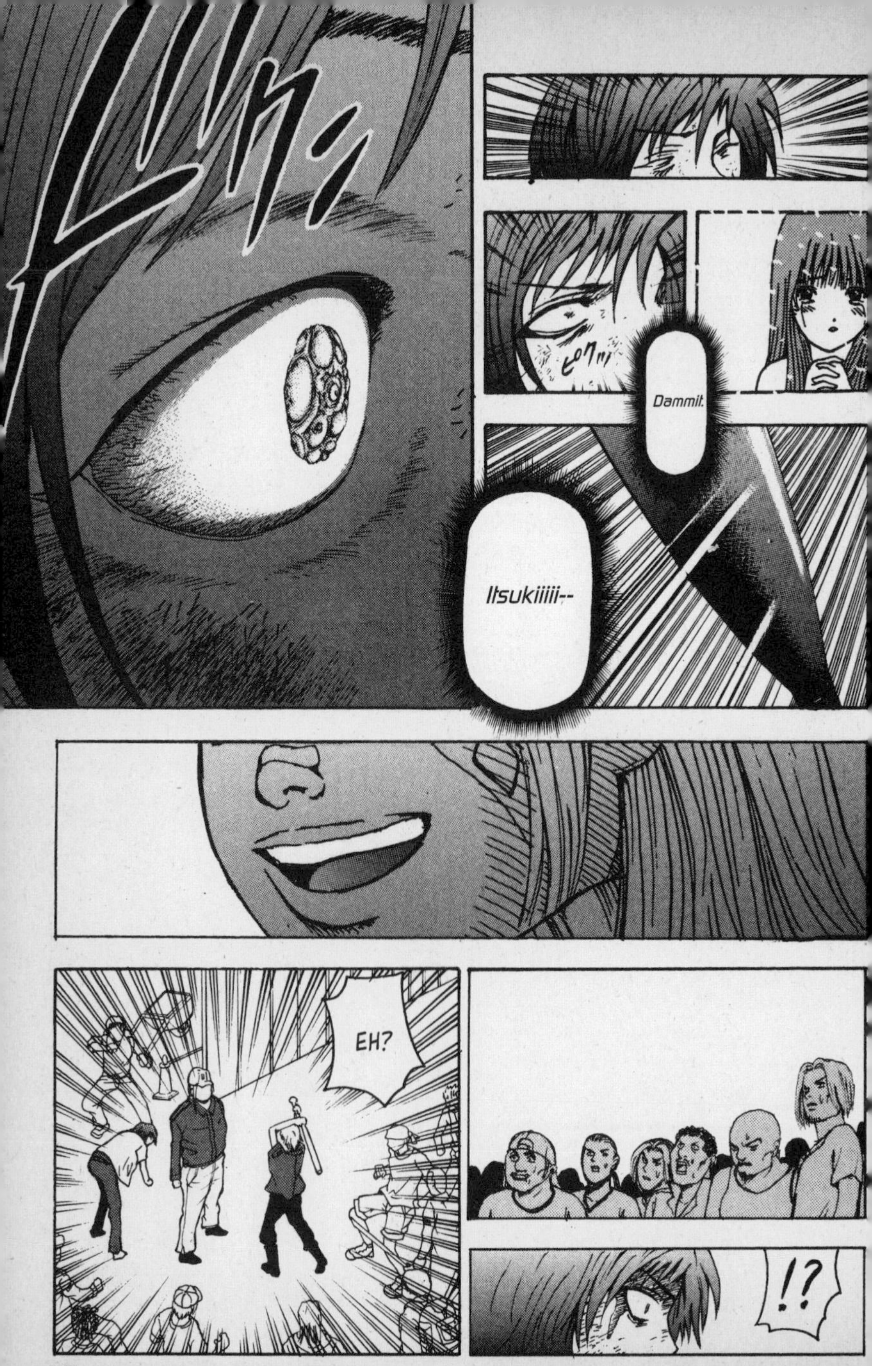
Dammit.
Itsukiiiii--
!?
EH?

Who the hell is this guy?
HEY, WHAT DO YOU THINK YOU'RE DOING?!
THIS DON'T CONCERN YOU.
LOOKING TO SHARE A GRAVE WITH HIM?
YOU IDIOTS.
I JUST SAVED YOU DIMWITS.
YOU WHAT?!
THAT BAT YOU TRIED TO HIT HIM WITH.
TAKE A GOOD LOOK AT IT.
WHAT'S HE TALKING ABOU--?
HUH??!

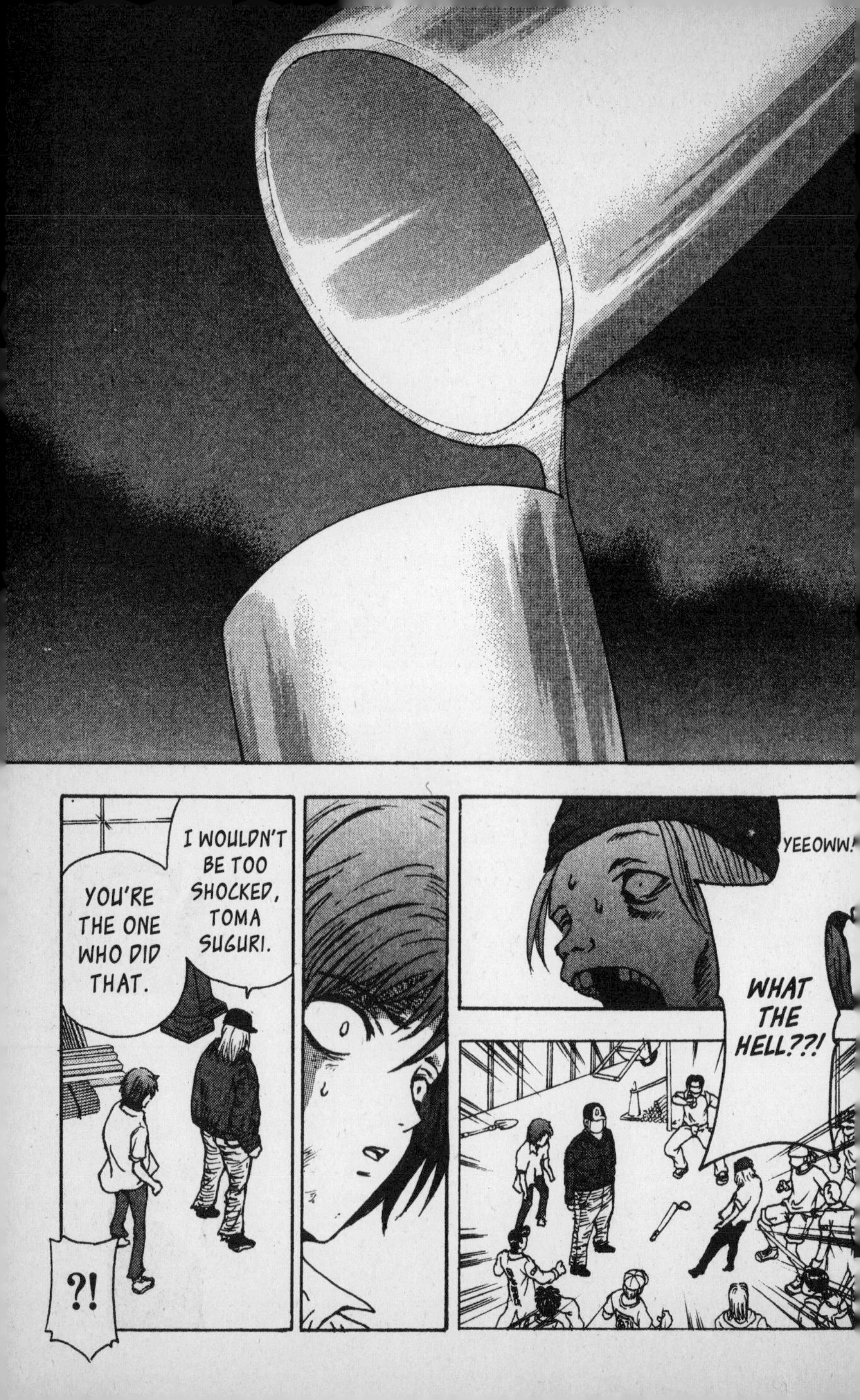
YEEOWW!
WHAT THE HELL??!
I WOULDN'T BE TOO SHOCKED, TOMA SUGURI.
YOU'RE THE ONE WHO DID THAT.
?!

End of EPISODE 3 - Enter: The Hardcore Wanderer

My right eye?!
The power of Codon?!
YOU GOTTA BE CAREFUL WITH CODON.
DANGEROUS WEAPON. COULD FRY SOMEONE BEFORE YOU EVEN KNOW IT.
LOOK, WHO ARE YOU?
ME?

# EPISODE 4 - The Soldier Teacher [Axel Potter - Part 2]

!!
OW.
ALL THAT GARBAGE ISN'T GOING TO CHANGE NOTHING.
YOU HEAR ME, FAT ASS?
THERE. NOW MAYBE YOU TWO'LL STOP BABBLING ABOUT ALL THAT BULLSHIT.
ガッ
YOUR MAGIC TRICKS AIN'T GONNA DO JACK.

WE DON'T SCARE SO EASY.
SEE?!
OOHHPH...
HA HA HA!
DOWN LIKE A SACK OF BRICKS.
HE WAS A LIGHTWEIGHT FROM THE START.
He did go down pretty quick.
I just assumed all the gladiators were tough guys like Karma.
HEY!
YOU!
THAT'S ENOUGH, KIDDIES.
HE'S A HEFTY BOY. TRY PICKING ON SOMEONE YOUR OWN SIZE.
WHAT?!
Grrr!

I GOT A FEW QUESTIONS FOR THIS GUY.
YOU IMPAIRED HIS ABILITY TO ANSWER, SO I'M NOT TOO FREAKIN' HAPPY.
JACK-ASS...
YOU GOT A LOT OF NERVE!
YOU'RE THE ONE THAT STARTED THIS FIGHT IN THE FIRST PLACE!
HUH?
OH YEAH, YOU'RE *RIGHT*.
HEY, BIG GUY.
YOU BETTER MOVE ASIDE.
REST UP YOUR MOUTH, 'CAUSE WHEN I'M DONE MOPPIN' UP THESE GUYS, I WANT SOME ANSWERS.
MY...
WHAT'S WRONG? CAN'T GET UP?
MM...
...MMMY...

MY...
...
MOUTH
...
GROSS!

HAHAHA! NOW, THAT'S COMEDY!
WHAT'S WRONG WITH YOU, DUDE? YOU GOT A SCREW LOOSE?!
PLEASE! MR. POLICEMAN! WE HAVE TO HURRY!
BUT YOU SAID MORE THAN 30 BIKER PUNKS, RIGHT?
I CAN'T DO NOTHIN' ABOUT IT 'TIL BACKUP SHOWS.
JUST PEDAL! TOMA COULD BE KILLED IN THE TIME YOU'RE WASTING.
ちりん
ちりん
YOU KNOW, YOU RUN PRETTY GOOD FOR SOMEONE SO CHESTY.
PLEASE, TOMA!
HANG ON, WE'RE COMING!!
HERE!
THIS IS THE PLACE!

TOMA!!
HUH?

WHAT THE--?
A-A SUICIDE...?!
EEEEK!
HE...
HE-HE ISN'T... DEAD?
AHHH !!
むくっ

オオオオ
YEEEAAAAAAAHHHHHHH!
オオオオオ
CRAZY, DUDE!
HE DROPPED THREE STORIES, AND HE'S STILL GOING!
WHAT A FREAK!

WHAT IS ALL THIS?
ウオオオ
YOU, KID.
WHAT'S GOING ON HERE?
GULP
Yikes, the fuzz!
オオオオオ
WELL, UM, THAT BIG GUY OVER THERE...
...HE GOT HIS TEETH KNOCKED OUT, BUT HE'S ALL SMILING ABOUT IT.
SO, EVERYONE'S, LIKE, CHEERING AND SAYING HOW TOUGH HE IS.
AND GETTING ALL EXCITED AND STUFF.
AND SAYING, LIKE, "LET'S SEE WHAT ELSE YOU CAN DO..."
YAH!
HOORAY!
SO HE DIVES FROM THE THIRD STORY.
MORE!
NAIRN
CHEER ME ON MORE!

HWAH HA HA HA HA HA HA!!
YOU'RE A REAL FUNNY GUY!
THAT'S MY BUSINESS. TO MAKE PEOPLE HAPPY.
GLAD I'M DOING A GOOD JOB. ♡
YOUR BUSINESS?! WHAT LINE OF WORK YOU IN?
AH, WELL, THAT'S A LONG STORY...
MAN.
I FIGURED ALL THE GLADIATORS WOULD BE THESE HOT-SHOTS LIKE THAT KARMA GUY.
WHO KNEW THERE WERE MORONS LIKE YOU IN THE MIX, TOO? HA HA HA!
HEY, TOMA!
YOU'RE A PRETTY BIG MORON YOURSELF, YOU KNOW.
GUESS SO. TAKING ON A WHOLE ARMY LIKE THIS.
WHAT THE HECK HAPPENED ...?
LOOKS LIKE THEY'RE ALL GETTING ALONG TO ME.
SO I'LL BE GOING.
I...
HEY...

HUH? TEACH?
WHAT ARE YOU DOING HERE?
WHAT AM I DOING HERE?
WHAT AM I DOING HERE?
I-I...
I- I...
WHO IS THIS GENTLEMAN?
He looks like a bear.
YOU MEAN HIM?
OH, HIS NAME'S AXEL. WE'RE BUDS.
YO, AXEL.
MEET MY TEACHER. SHE'S THE PHYS ED LIAISON, MISS HIMEKAWA.
ドキ
ドキ
ドキ

WOW, THIS IS YOUR PLACE, MISS HIMEKAWA?
ドキ
ドキ
ドキ
LOOK, YOU DON'T HAVE TO WORRY WITH ALL THE BANDAGES AND STUFF.
It's just a few scrapes.
I DO HAVE TO WORRY.
YOU'RE SUCH A CHILD, WOULDN'T EVEN LET ME TAKE YOU TO THE HOSPITAL.
OKAY.
YOU'RE NEXT, MR. AXEL.
AND WHEN I'M FINISHED HERE, WE DEFINITELY NEED TO SEE A DENTIST ABOUT THOSE TEETH.
NOW, THIS MAY HURT A BIT.
OH, UH...
FORGET THE TEETH.
THEY WERE ALL FAKES ANYHOW.
HUH?

YOU SEE, I'M A PROFESSIONAL WRESTLER BY TRADE.
I GET PAID TO TAKE BEATINGS.
TEETH DON'T LAST LONG IN MY LINE OF WORK.
A p-professional wrestler?!
OH, THAT'S SO EXCITING!
I'M A HUGE FAN!
I LOVE WATCHING WRESTLING!
AND EVERY DAY I READ THE SPORTS PAGES!
Wha--? You're kidding!
WHICH LEAGUE DO YOU PLAY WITH?
N-NOT THE WW...?!
NAH, IT'S A...UH...MUCH SMALLER ONE.
WE JUST STARTED OUR TOUR.
I SEE.
SO THAT'S WHY YOU JUST SHUT UP AND TOOK THAT BEATING.
YOU DIDN'T WANT TO GO OFF AND HURT SOMEONE.
EXACTLY.
FOR THE SAME REASON YOU DIDN'T BRING YOUR WOODEN SWORD ALONG.

I'M JUST GLAD WE GOT OUT OF THERE...
...WITHOUT ANYONE GETTING HURT.
Hmm...
ARE THOSE, LIKE, KARMA'S ORDERS?
That guy called me a monkey and acted like he wanted to kill me.
...
ピルルルルッ
OH! THE PHONE.
EXCUSE ME.
LISTEN, AXEL.
WHAT YOU SAID BEFORE...
...ABOUT TRAINING ME AND STUFF...

HEY!
WE DIDN'T COME HERE TO PLAY WITH PEOPLE'S UNDERWEAR!
ドキ ドキ
THIS IS ONE OF THE NEWEST SECURITY MANAGEMENT TECHNIQUES OUT OF THE U.S.
YOU CAN TELL A LOT ABOUT A PERSON BY THEIR PANTIES, EVALUATE WHETHER OR NOT SHE'S SOME WEIRDO WHO BROUGHT US HERE TO RAPE US...
GIVE ME THOSE, YOU CRAZY FOOL!
MARI
TOMA...
I'M NOT SURE IF YOU REALLY UNDERSTAND KARMA AND WHAT HE'S TRYING TO DO.
UNDERSTAND HIM?!
THE GUY KIDNAPPED THE SWEETEST GIRL I EVER MET! PLUS HE PLUCKED MY EYE OUT!
YEAH, I HEARD THERE WAS SOME FEATHER RUFFLING BETWEEN YOU TWO.
AND THAT ITSUKI AIZAWA WAS CAUGHT IN THE MIDDLE.
BUT LISTEN. AIZAWA NEEDS TRAINING TOO. THAT'S A FACT.
EVERYTHING KARMA DOES, HE DOES WITH ONE PURPOSE.
TO GET OUR TEAM READY SO WE CAN DEFEND THE WORLD.

IF IT WEREN'T FOR KARMA, WE WOULDN'T HAVE A CHANCE.
WE'D ALL BE PART OF A GALACTIC SMORGASBORD. NO QUESTION.
HMPH.
AXEL, YOU SURPRISE ME.
BELIEVING ALL THOSE FAIRYTALES.
AT YOUR AGE.
HEY! WHAT THE HELL ARE YOU DOING NOW?!
RUSTLE
ピクッ
HMM?
YOU FIND SOMETHING?
プル
プル
OH...
WELL, AFTER ALL, SHE *IS* 25, YOU KNOW.
NOT SO SURPRISING IF THERE'S A BOYFRIEND OR TWO...
キャッ
キャッ
MASAHIRO! YOU BEHAVE YOURSELF!

NOW YOU'RE EAVESDROPPING??! WITH A GLASS?!
SOME GLADIATOR!
The guy seem a little overly interested in Miss Hime-kawa.
Wonder what he really came here for.
Then again, she is a good-looking lady.
Guess it's not impossible he's just fallen for her. (After all, she's got a nice rack.)
Hmph. Love at first sight.
YES, I KNOW.
BUT I CAN'T...
Funny thing.
I haven't known Itsuki for long at all, now that I think about it.
But somehow, the longer we're apart, the more gaga I seem to get.

Shoot, if it hadn't been for blondie...
...I could have been with her for those three days.
HUH?
日 月 火
1 2 3 4 5
8 9
15 16
Did I just say "three days"...?
Yikes!
バタ バタ
ガチャ
TOMA?! HELLO?!
ゴロ ゴロ
108

IT'S ALL I HAVE.
ペル・バレエスクール
オーディション
終了しました
BALLET'S MY MOST IMPORTANT THING.
MODERN BALLET. ENDLESS PRACTICE.
I'VE BEEN DOING IT FOR TEN YEARS NOW.
'TIL FINALLY I BEGAN TO HAVE A LITTLE FAITH IN MYSELF.
SO THIS AUDITION IS REALLY IMPORTANT TO ME.
終了し
DON'T WORRY. YOU'LL PASS.
I'LL PROTECT YOU.

* Ballet School - Auditions Have Ended

I'LL PROTECT YOU.
choke
SOME HELP!
I'M ALL TALK!
I MADE A PROMISE TO HER.
ONE PROMISE, AND I COULDN'T EVEN KEEP IT...
DAMMIT!
HOW AM I SUPPOSED TO GET THAT GIRL BACK?!
HOW AM I SUPPOSED TO DEFEAT KARMA??! TELL ME THAT!!

IF YOU WANT ACCESS TO TAO ...
...YOU HAVE TO USE THE CODON.
I don't even know how to get back there.
Back to that world. Back to that bizarre place.
U.S
AXEL...
THE CODON INSIDE OF YOU IS STILL YOUNG, LIKE A NEWBORN INFANT.
WITH THE RIGHT TRAINING, YOU CAN GROW INTO IT.
MANIPULATE IT LIKE IT WAS A NATURAL PART OF YOU.
BUT, REMEMBER, THE CODON'S NO ORDINARY WEAPON.
IT'S A LINK TO THE SOUL OF ITS POSSESSOR.
IT'S TRIGGERED BY SIGNALS INSIDE THE BRAIN, TO PRODUCE A SPECIAL CONCENTRATED FIELD OF ENERGY THAT TAKES SHAPE AND GROWS LIKE ITS OWN ARTIFICIAL LIFE-FORM.

WHEN THAT HAPPENS, YOU'LL FIND THAT THE CODON IS MORE THAN JUST THE ULTIMATE WEAPON.
IT'S A DOORWAY THAT CAN TRANSPORT YOU TO TAO ANYTIME YOU LIKE. IF YOU USE IT PROPERLY.
WILL IT?!
YOU'RE SAYING I CAN GO THERE ANYTIME I WANT?!
I can go help Itsuki!!
I can go!!
PLEASE, AXEL.
YOU'VE GOT TO TELL ME HOW THIS THING WORKS!
I'LL--
I'LL DO WHATEVER IT TAKES!
LIKE I SAID.
THAT'S THE WHOLE REASON I CAME HERE.

Tao
KARMA.
WE'D LIKE TO KNOW THE REASON THAT YOU SENT AXEL POTTER TO MAKE CONTACT WITH TOMA SUGURI.
TRAINING, OF COURSE.
I THINK IT'S ABUNDANTLY CLEAR. ♡
YOUR INTENT IS TO HAVE MR. TOMA ELIMINATED UNDER THE GUISE OF TRAINING HIM. ♡
EVEN IF THAT WERE THE CASE...
...YOU HAVE NO AUTHORITY TO INVOLVE YOURSELF IN WHAT HAPPENS DURING MY TRAINING EXERCISES.
PERHAPS NOT.
BLWIP
BUT AS JUDGING OFFICIALS, WE NEED TO STAY ABREAST OF ANY POTENTIAL VIOLATIONS. ♡

PLEASE, AXEL.
YOU'VE GOT TO TELL ME HOW THIS THING WORKS!
I'LL DO WHATEVER IT TAKES!
HA!
PASSIONATE AS USUAL, I SEE. ♡
THAT POOR BOY SURE WASTES A LOT OF ENERGY.
HMPH...
I ASSUME YOU'VE HEARD?
MISS ITSUKI AIZAWA...
...THAT CRAZED MONKEY IS TRYING TO GET BACK TO SAVE YOU.

I DON'T THINK HE EVEN KNOWS WHAT HE'S GOING TO DO WHEN HE GETS HERE.
BUT SUDDENLY HE THINKS HE'S YOUR KNIGHT IN SHINING ARMOR.
HOW DOES IT FEEL TO BE THE PRINCESS?
DON'T YOU WORRY.
THAT MONKEY'S NOT GOING TO MAKE IT.
I'VE GIVEN AXEL THE ORDER TO...
...KILL HIM AND GET IT OVER WITH.
......
AXEL'S LIKE YOU, YOU SEE.
サラッ

ITSUKI AIZAWA AND AXEL POTTER.
BOTH SOLDIERS. YOU WORK FOR ME.

YEAH, COME ON!
SO, WHAT DO I DO TO TRAIN, AXEL?!
ウズウズ
YOU'LL BE SURPRISED. LIKE ME WITH KENDO. I'M A QUICK STUDY.
...
ゾクッ
A... AXEL ...?
What the hell?
He's changed all of a sudden!
Something about his vibe.
He feels... dangerous!!
......
WELL, NORMALLY IT TAKES TIME TO GROW INTO THE CODON.
TO RUSH IT IS GOING TO TAKE AN ENORMOUS AMOUNT OF POWER.
BUT LET ME TELL YOU A SECRET.
THERE'S ONE WAY TO MASTER THE CODON ALL AT ONCE.

THAT'S WHEN YOU'RE FIGHTING FOR YOUR LIFE.
End of EPISODE 4 - The Soldier Teacher

# EPISODE 5 - Karma's Assassin [Axel Potter - Part 3]

A-AXEL ...?!
What's happened to him?
So weird.
All of a sudden...
...it's like he's out to ice me!
パシャ

He-He's playing for real!

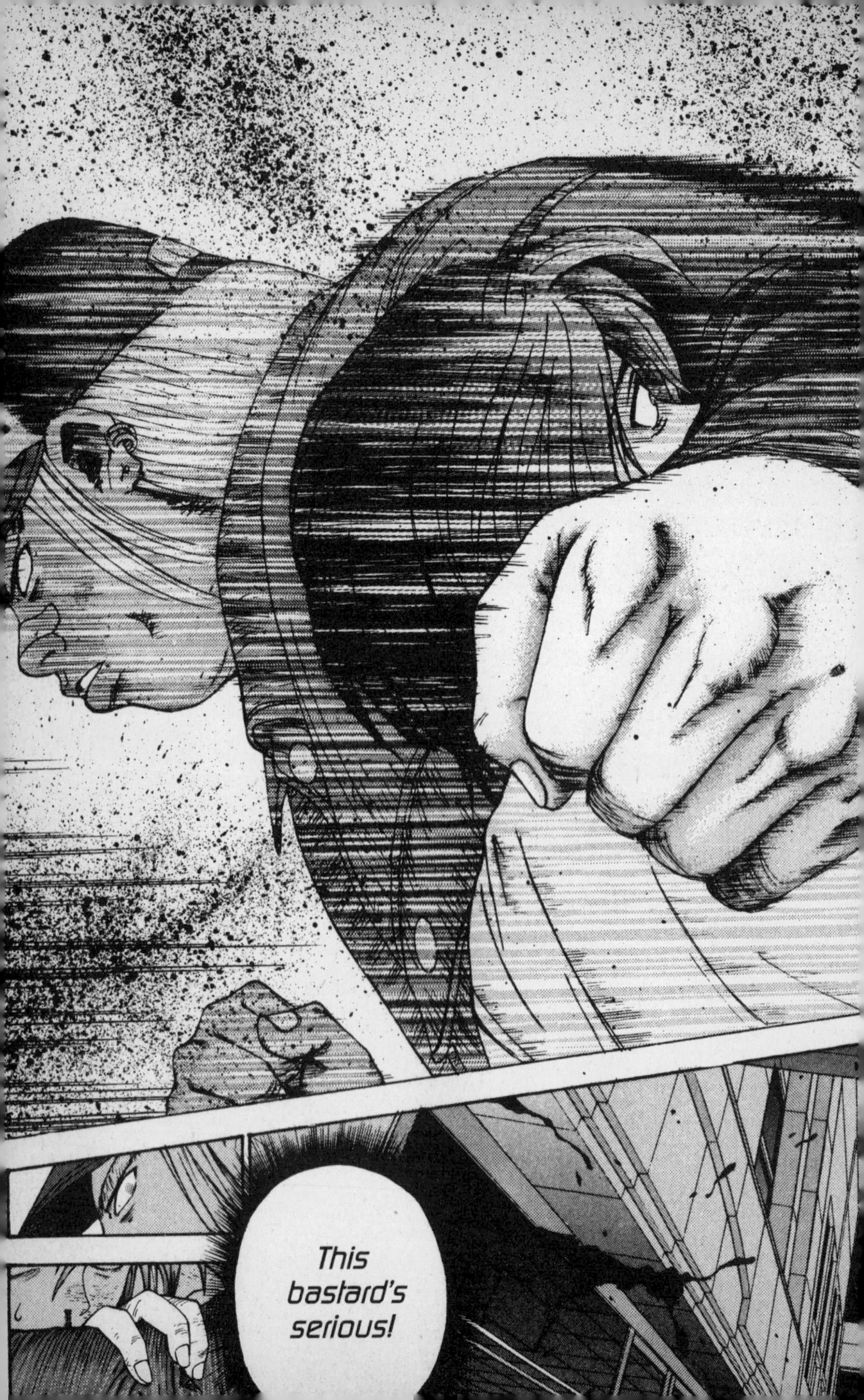
This bastard's serious!

He wants to kill me!
He was so friendly earlier today.
Dowww!
Doof!

We were a team!
I'M JUST GLAD WE GOT OUT OF THERE...
...WITHOUT ANYONE GETTING HURT.
We even stole the teacher's panties together!!
He totally won my trust.
EVERYTHING KARMA DOES, HE DOES WITH ONE PURPOSE.
TO GET OUR TEAM READY SO WE CAN DEFEND THE WORLD.
TOMA ...
I'M NOT SURE IF YOU REALLY UNDERSTAND KARMA AND WHAT HE'S TRYING TO DO.
And now...
...he's trying to take me out!
BOFF

Karma...
Karma?!

bwuk
I FINALLY FIGURED IT OUT.
YOU'RE HIS ASSASSIN, AREN'T YOU?
Bright idea!
IT'S ABOUT TIME HE WISED UP. MOST PEOPLE WOULD BE A BIT MORE CAREFUL IN THE FIRST PLACE.
Plots have twists, you know.
WELL, YES, HE'S SIMPLE. BUT THAT'S WHAT MAKES HIM CUTE.

OKAY, SO YOU'RE HIS BOY.
BUT HOW COME? TELL ME THAT.
HAS HE GOT SOME DIRT ON YOU OR WHAT?
......
MARINE
YOU CAN'T FOOL ME. YOU TRY TO LOOK ALL SPOOKY.
BUT YOU'RE REALLY JUST A PUPPY DOG.
I GET A GOOD-GUY AURA OFF OF YOU.

hand↑

AND YET YOU COME HERE TO TRY TO SNUFF ME OUT.
I KNOW THERE'S GOT TO BE A POWERFULLY GOOD REASON FOR THAT. KARMA'S GOT YOU BY THE BALLS.
ハッ
ブン ブン
NEVER MIND! I DON'T WANT TO KNOW!
DON'T EVEN TELL ME!
That was close.
If I let him spill his guts, he'll probably get me all teary-eyed.
Then how am I supposed to treat him as the enemy?
Yeah, yeah. He's a good guy.
But he's trying to kill me, dammit!
Got to keep focused on the enemy, take him down.
If I don't...

...IF I LET HIM PUNCH MY TICKET...
...THEN WHO THE HELL'S GOING TO SAVE ITSUKI?!
ITSUKI AIZAWA, ITSUKI AIZAWA. IT'S ALL HE EVER THINKS ABOUT.
MAKES YOU WANT TO CRY! TEE-HEE! ♡
BUT HE WAS ONLY WITH HER FOR TWO OR THREE HOURS AT MOST.
ENOUGH OF A SIMPLETON TO BEAT TWENTY-BILLION-TO-ONE ODDS.
IS THAT ENOUGH TO GET A PERSON THIS EMOTIONAL?
....

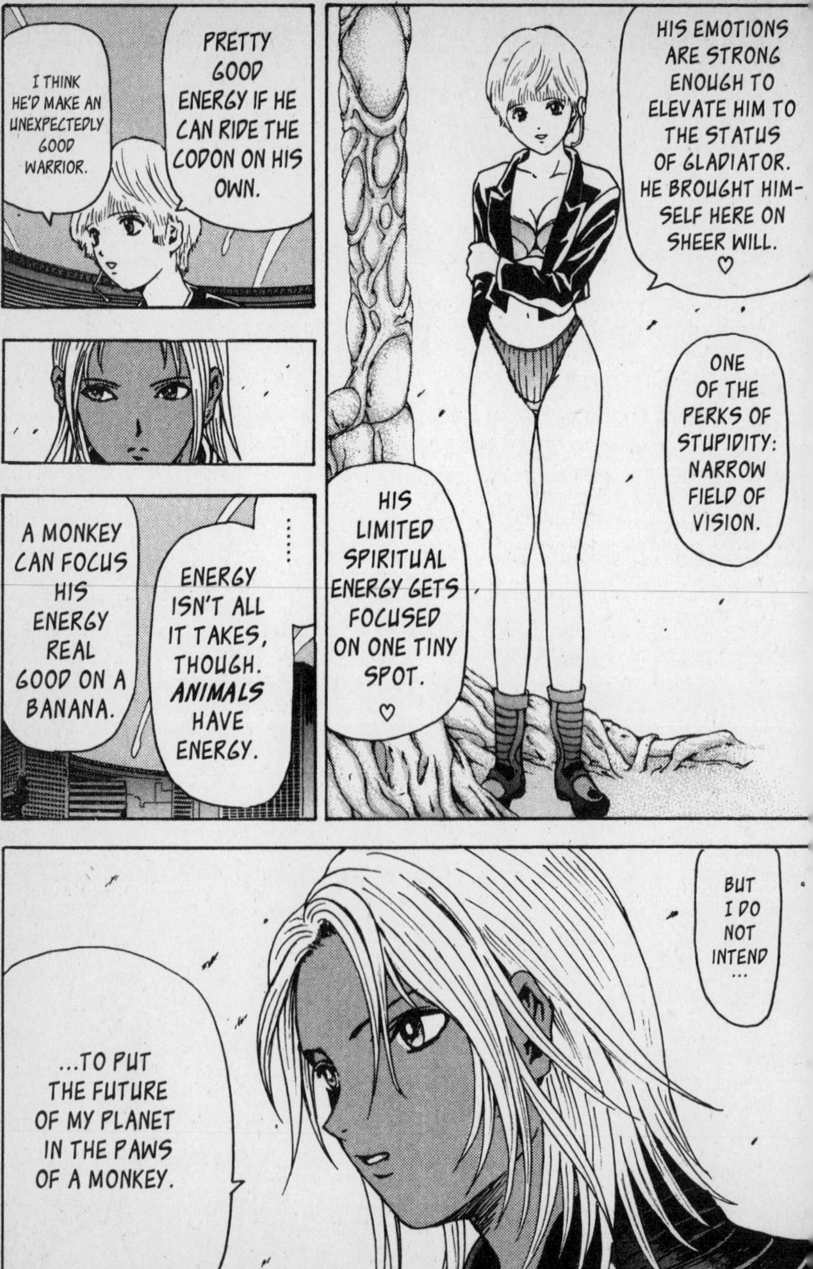
HIS EMOTIONS ARE STRONG ENOUGH TO ELEVATE HIM TO THE STATUS OF GLADIATOR. HE BROUGHT HIM-SELF HERE ON SHEER WILL. ♡
ONE OF THE PERKS OF STUPIDITY: NARROW FIELD OF VISION.
HIS LIMITED SPIRITUAL ENERGY GETS FOCUSED ON ONE TINY SPOT. ♡
PRETTY GOOD ENERGY IF HE CAN RIDE THE CODON ON HIS OWN.
I THINK HE'D MAKE AN UNEXPECTEDLY GOOD WARRIOR.
......
ENERGY ISN'T ALL IT TAKES, THOUGH. ***ANIMALS*** HAVE ENERGY.
A MONKEY CAN FOCUS HIS ENERGY REAL GOOD ON A BANANA.
BUT I DO NOT INTEND...
...TO PUT THE FUTURE OF MY PLANET IN THE PAWS OF A MONKEY.

Eep-eep!
ボリボリ
TEE-HEE.
YOU KNOW.
HE JUST SAID SOMETHING PROFOUNDLY CLEVER. I WONDER IF HE REALIZES IT.
GIVE HIM A WHILE. THOSE BROODING TYPES NEVER LEAVE STONES UNTURNED FOR LONG.
ボリ
ボリ
ボリ

...I DON'T WANT TO DO IT.
I DON'T WANT TO KILL YOU.
U.S
TOMA...
Let's go.
WHATSA MATTER? LOST YOUR FIGHT?
Come on, you want to take me down, right?
IN FACT, I DON'T WANT TO KILL ANYBODY.
I'M A PROFESSIONAL WRESTLER.
MY JOB IS TO MAKE PEOPLE HAPPY.
AND YET...
I ORDER YOU TO KILL SUGURI TOMA...
...AXEL POTTER.
I'M NO KILLER.

AND HERE IS THE REASON...
THE WAY KARMA EXPLAINED IT, IF ALL THAT STUFF IS TRUE...
...THEN THIS GUY'LL PUT OUR WHOLE TEAM AT RISK. EVERYTHING.
HUH?
What's happening?
This doesn't feel right.
In fact, I'm getting some pretty creepy vibes!
IF KARMA WAS ON THE LEVEL, THE TEAM COULD LOSE, AND OUR WHOLE PLANET BECOMES A BIG BUFFET TABLE...SO...

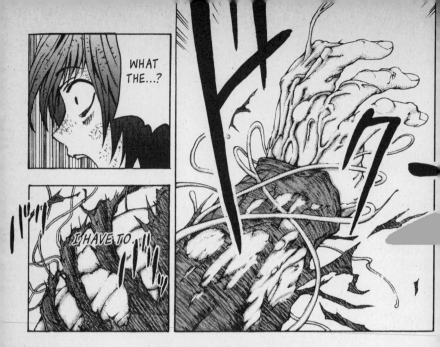

WHAT THE...?
I HAVE TO.
I'M THE PROTECTOR!
I CAN'T AFFORD TO LOSE!
MARINE
NO... FUCKING... WAY!

I must kill Toma Suguri.
MUST KILL HIM!

Rrrraarrrgggh!!!
KILL HIM!
TAKE A LOOK, ITSUKI. YOU SHOULD SEE THIS.
THE MONKEY'S LAST STAND.

DIFFERENT PEOPLE USE THE CODON IN DIFFERENT WAYS. THEY MOLD IT IN LINE WITH THEIR CHARACTER.
SEE AXEL'S CODON.
THE WAY HIS MUSCLES EXPAND.
YOU...
YOU...
IT ACTIVATES HIS PITUITARY GLANDS, AND THE LYMPH NODES UNDER HIS ARMS MAKE HIS BLOOD VESSELS SWELL AND THROB...
...UNTIL THE CODON *BECOMES HIM*--HIS ENTIRE BODY.

AXEL ALLOWS THE CODON TO TAKE HIM OVER, TO MANIFEST ITSELF THROUGH HIM.
JUST AS YOU SEE HERE.

It's happened again.
Head filled with thoughts of Aizawa. Eyes burning.
PHEW...
Did I kill him?
Dammit, Axel!
You were a really good guy, man...

FOR REAL?
YOU STILL OKAY...?
WHOA...
NOOOOO!!
INDEED.
AXEL'S CODON GIVES HIM HIS GREATEST TECHNIQUE.

The Human A-Bomb!

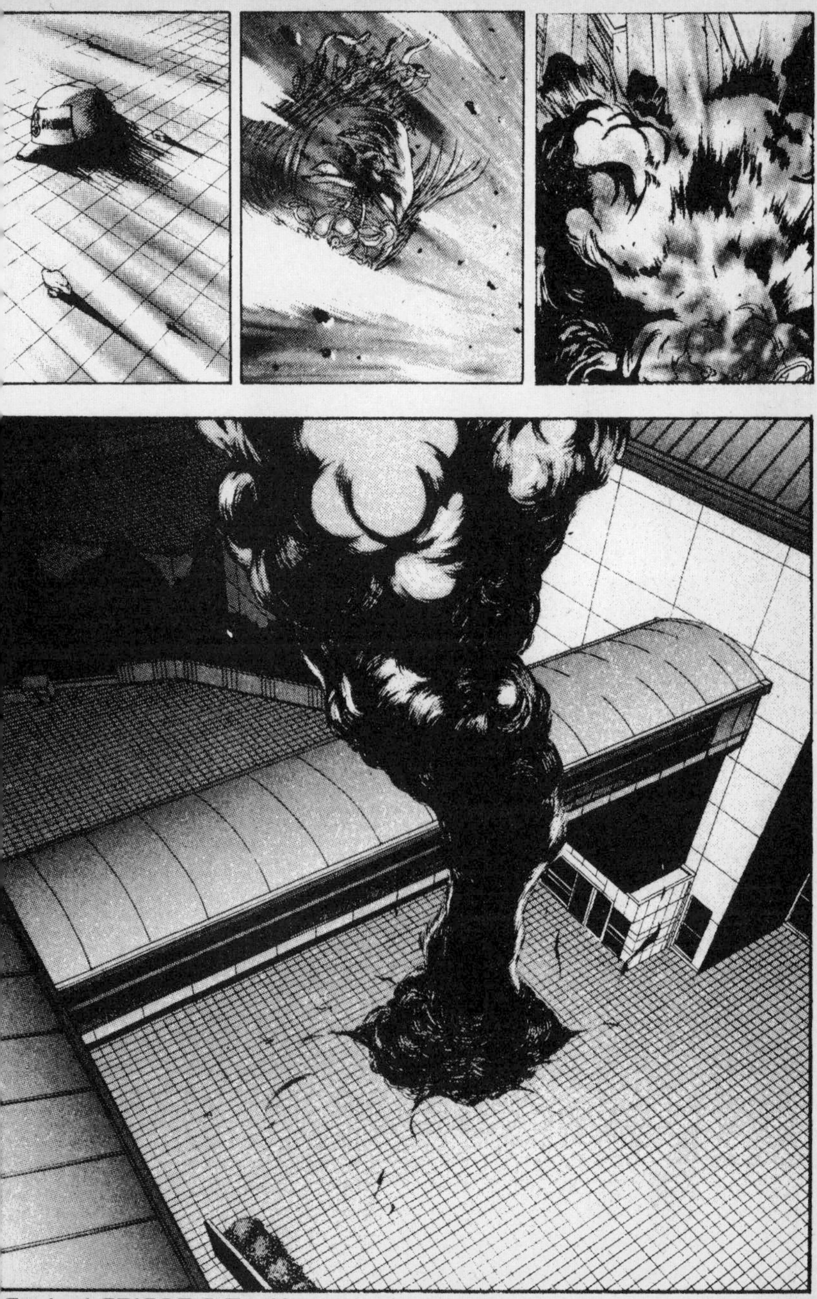

End of EPISODE 5 - Karma's Assassin

# EPISODE 6 - One Last Test
## [Axel Potter - Part 4]

AXEL...
YOU MAY HAVE A BABY FACE, BUT IT'S THE KIND NO ONE WANTS TO ROOT FOR.
THAT'S WHAT MY PROMOTER TOLD ME, JUST BEFORE MY FIRST FIGHT.
THIS MUG MEANT I COULD GET WORK, BUT I'D HAVE TO PLAY THE BAD GUY.

AND THEN THE PROMOTER PUT TWO GRAND IN MY HAND.
BUT I GOT BACK UP AND DID IT FOR A WEEK.
AND IT WAS THAT VERY FIGHT WHERE I BUSTED MY NOSE AND LOST MY THREE FRONT TEETH.
I SENT IT TO MY MOM.
I WISHED I COULD'VE HAND DELIVERED IT, BUT BY THEN MY FACE LOOKED LIKE A MONSTER'S. I COULDN'T LET HER SEE WHAT HAD HAPPENED TO HER BABY BOY.
WE LIVED IN A TRAILER PARK, YOU SEE. WHAT YOU CALL YOUR WHITE-TRASH NEIGHBORHOOD.
AS SOON AS SHE GOT THAT MONEY, SHE SENT ME SUCH A JOYOUS LETTER OF THANKS THAT...
WELL, THAT WAS FIVE YEARS AGO.
I'VE BEEN WRESTLING EVER SINCE.

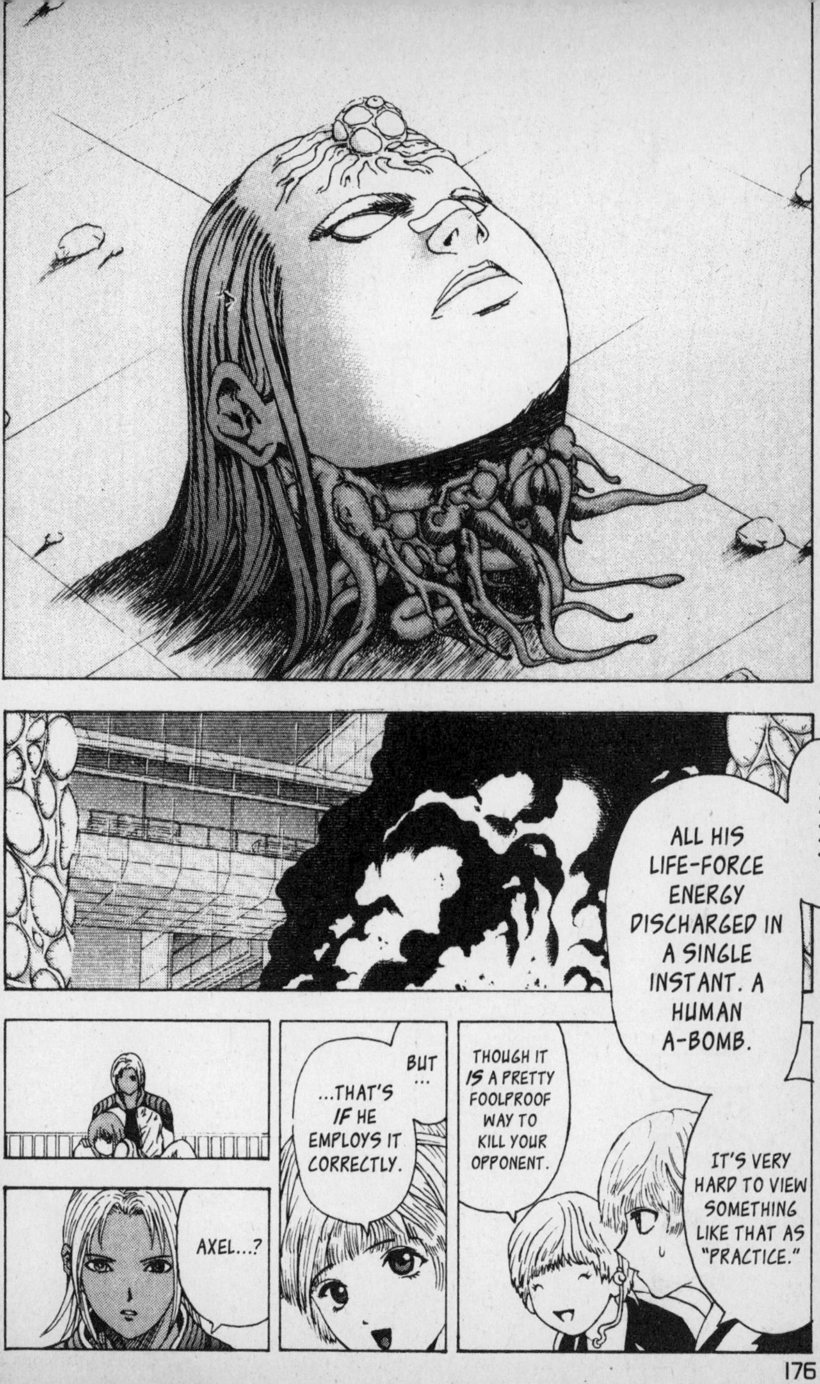
......
ALL HIS LIFE-FORCE ENERGY DISCHARGED IN A SINGLE INSTANT. A HUMAN A-BOMB.
IT'S VERY HARD TO VIEW SOMETHING LIKE THAT AS "PRACTICE."
THOUGH IT IS A PRETTY FOOLPROOF WAY TO KILL YOUR OPPONENT.
BUT ...
...THAT'S IF HE EMPLOYS IT CORRECTLY.
AXEL...?

NOOOO!!!
Ahhhh!
Grnt!
Egck!!
ズキン
ズキン

Just when he blew...
...I kicked back with everything I had.
pant
pant
A fraction of a second later, and I wouldn't have made it!!
H-horrible...
That was a real close one.
Doof...
へなあっ
HEY... AXEL... WAKE UP.
COME ON... ANSWER ME!
ズリッ
ズリッ

CRAZY BASTARD!
AN INSTANT BEFORE YOU BLEW UP...
...YOU LET GO OF ME.
IF YOU HADN'T, I'D HAVE NEVER BEEN ABLE TO KICK AWAY IN TIME.
I'D BE **DEAD** RIGHT NOW.
I CAN'T EVEN THANK YOU! CAN'T EVEN SQUARE THINGS UP!
I HATE THESE KIND OF GOODBYES!
Could it be...
He couldn't be...
ズルッ

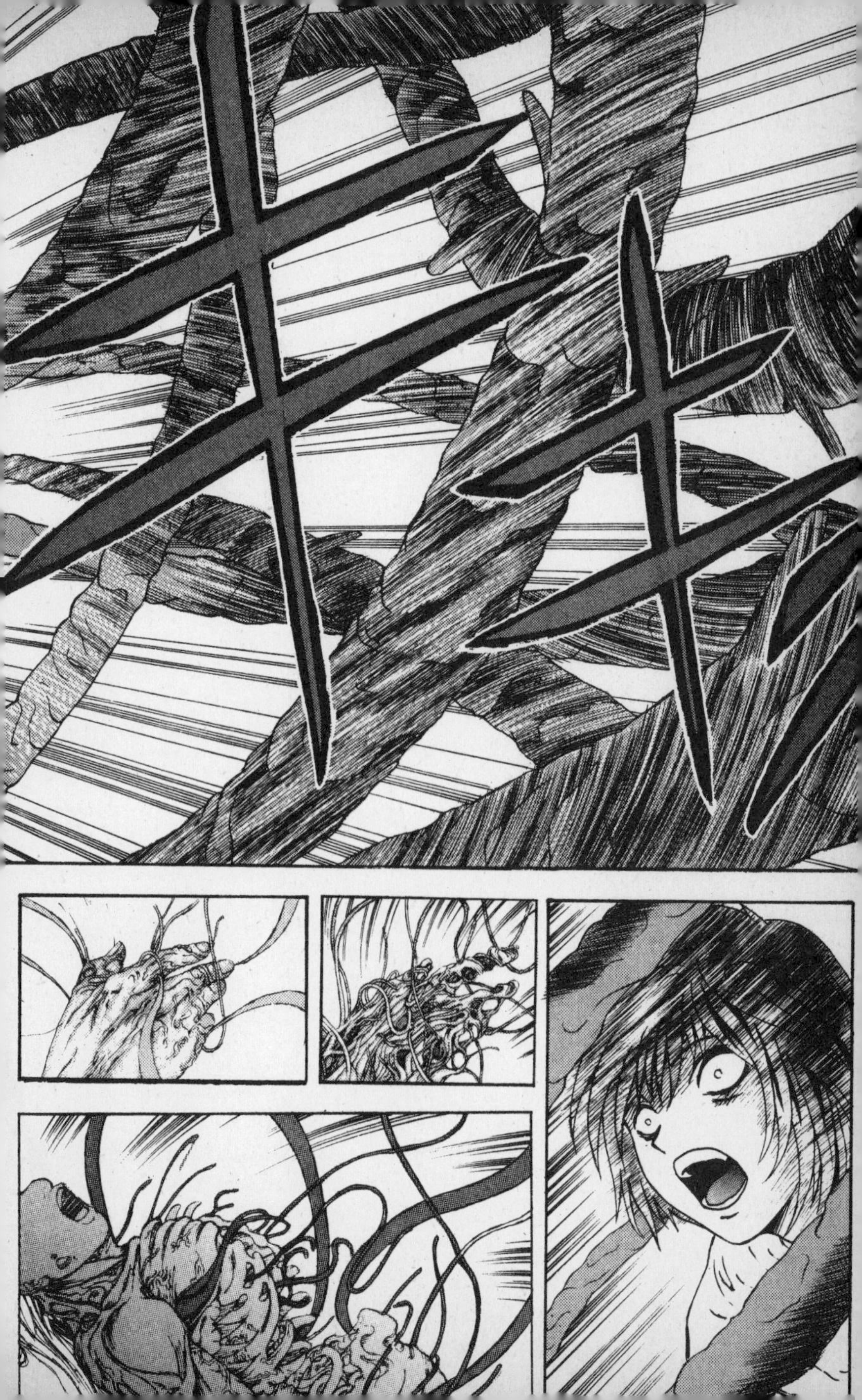

HE'S...
...COMING BACK TO LIFE?!

Dooff...
gasp
I don't care how tough the guy is, this is nuts!
Insane!
The guy's a walking zombie!

Calm down! Hold it together!
I've got this Codon thing too, right?!
I felt it just now. It's all in the timing.
Just got to find that sensation and hold on to it!
カッ

You're kidding!

This isn't going to work! Even if I put him down, he'll just rise from the dead again!
Plus he's does that kamikaze A-bomb thing!
A kendo sword against an A-bomb.
Like I've really got a chance!

He's too good.
Way too good!
Except...
...look at that face.
It's almost...
...almost like he...
Grrrrrrr!

ゼッ
ゼッ
カッ
ガシッ
ガッ
Aarrgg!
TOMA! WHY?!
ドッ
ガッ

WHY, TOMA?
WHY DO YOU KEEP COMING?!
STOP ALREADY!!
YOU DON'T HAVE A CHANCE OF BEATING ME!
YOU MUST KNOW THAT BY NOW!
PLEASE, TOMA...
...DON'T MAKE ME...

ALL FORM...
HE'S ATTACKING, BUT HIS HEART ISN'T IN IT.
THAT'S THE TROUBLE WITH THIS ONE.
HE CAN'T KILL.
SOME GLADIATOR. HE JUST GOES THROUGH THE MOTIONS.
Gulp...
I FEEL LIKE FRIGGING PUKING...
THIS ISN'T LIKE WHAT I DO WHEN I'M WRESTLING.
IN THAT RING, THERE'S STRICT RULES TO KEEP THINGS FROM GETTING OUT OF HAND.
OPPONENTS RESPECT ONE ANOTHER. THERE'S TRUST.
YOU'RE IN THERE FOR YOURSELF, BUT ALSO FOR THE OTHER GUY.
AND YOU'RE DOING IT FOR THE FANS. THERE'S A REASON FOR ALL THAT BLOOD AND SWEAT.

BUT OUT HERE THERE AREN'T ANY FANS.
I'M NOT ENTERTAINING ANYONE.
NOT GIVING ANYTHING.
I'M JUST A PREDATOR, A KILLER.
AXEL, LISTEN.
THIS FIGHT IS A TEST.
IF YOU CAN'T KILL THE MONKEY, I CAN'T USE YOU.
I'D RATHER HAVE YOU KILLED TOO.
AND OPEN YOUR SPACE FOR A NEW POTENTIAL GLADIATOR.

I thought so. I could tell by that look on your face.
Crazy bastard.
!!

YOU'RE NOT REALLY TRYING.
Every punch feels like...he's holding back.
If he were giving me all he had, I wouldn't still be standing here.
Crazy guy.
Even from the start...

...he's been treating me with kid gloves.
But I'm not a kid.
I DON'T GET THIS.
WHY DOESN'T HE FALL?
WHY DOESN'T HE JUST GO DOWN?
HE STILL WANTS MORE?!
I CAN'T TAKE MUCH MORE OF THIS!

IF I KEEP TRYING TO DO THIS, IT'S NOT HIS BODY THAT'S GOING TO COME APART.
IT'S MY HEART THAT'S GOING TO GIVE.
Aaaarrrrrhhhhggg!!
Freakin' scum bucket, I see him laughing at me.
The whole kid-glove bit.
He's toying with me. Getting his jollies watching me go, piece by piece!

End of EPISODE 6 - One Last Test

I want a weapon!
EPISODE 7 - Invoking the Codon [Axel Potter - Part 5]
To hell with Karma, and Axel too, for all I care!
I'll take them both down! I'll--

My weapon!

THAT WAS IT, TOMA! GAME OVER!
HMM. GUESS THAT'S THAT. ♡

DON'T WORRY, MONKEY.
I'LL TAKE GOOD CARE OF YOUR GIRL FOR YOU.

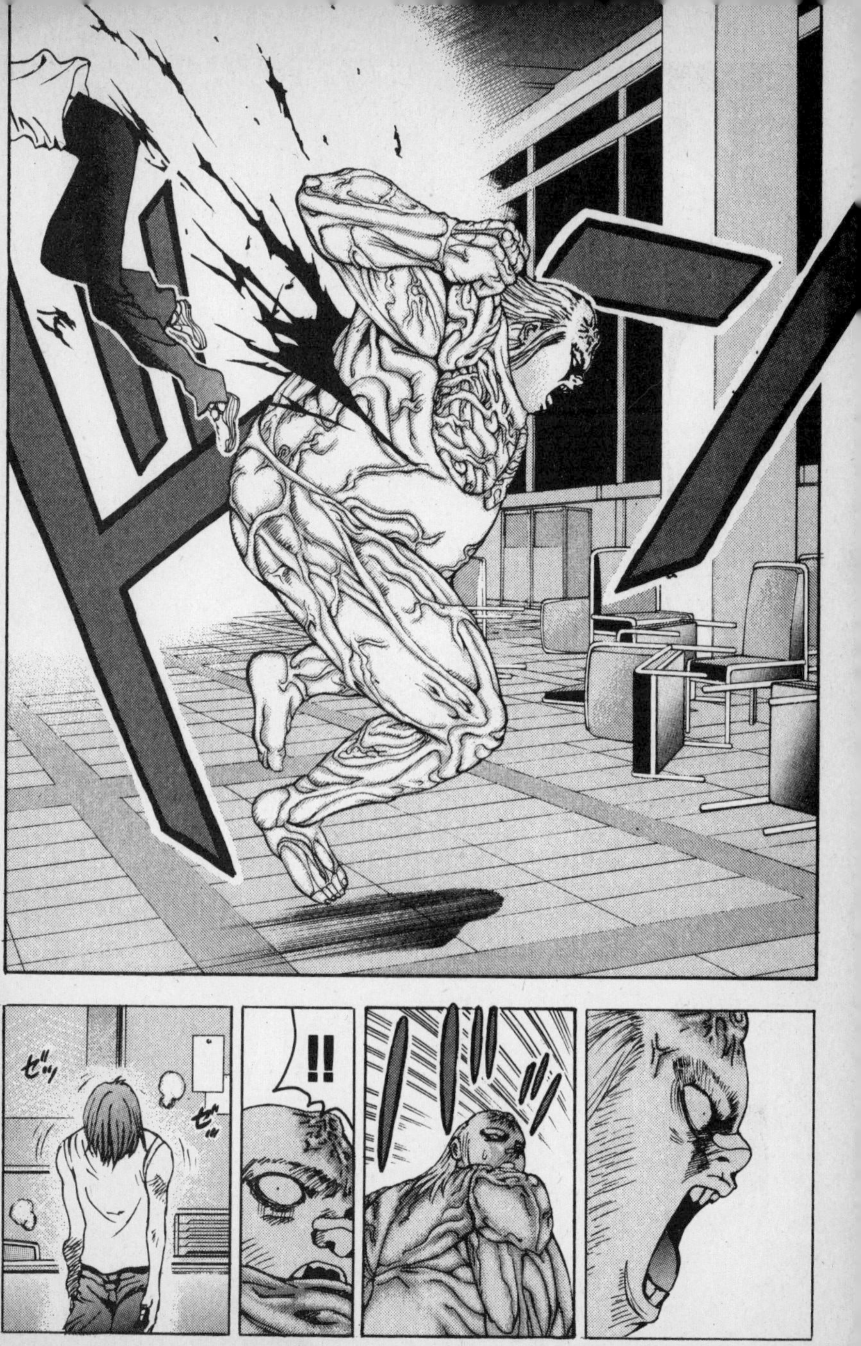
!!
ぜ
ぜ

......
MMMN-NMM...
!!
Whoa!
What am I doing?! Got to stay alert!
BUT...?!
I can't see out of my right eye!
Just great! My life's on the line and my eyesight's conking out!
?
Weird face. Like he's surprised at something, but what would he...?

HOLY FUCKING SHIT!!
WHAT THE HELL'S GOING ON?!
IS THIS PART OF THAT CODON DEAL?!
GIVE ME A FRIGGIN' BREAK!
TOMA'S CODON...
HE'S ALREADY DOING WEAPONS?!

I DON'T BELIEVE IT!
I WENT THROUGH HELL TRYING TO LEARN FROM KARMA HOW TO DO THAT!
AND THIS PALOOKA FIGURES IT OUT IN THREE DAYS?!
THE KID'S A GENIUS!
A STUPID GENIUS!
GREAT, SO NOW MY ARM'S A SWORD...
HOW AM I SUPPOSED TO MAKE TIME WITH ITSUKI LOOKING LIKE THIS?!

BUT HE STILL CAN'T BEAT ME!
YIKES!
QUIT BEING A CREEP!
LET'S AT LEAST TRY TO TALK THIS OVER!
KEEP IT UP, AXEL.
I'VE TRAINED YOU TO BE A BRAVE GLADIATOR.
THE LEAST YOU CAN DO IS SQUASH THAT MONKEY WITH-OUT WORRYING ABOUT IT.

AH!
WHOA!
This is no good! I can only see out of one eye!
I can't dodge him!
Guess that means...

...I'll have to charge him!

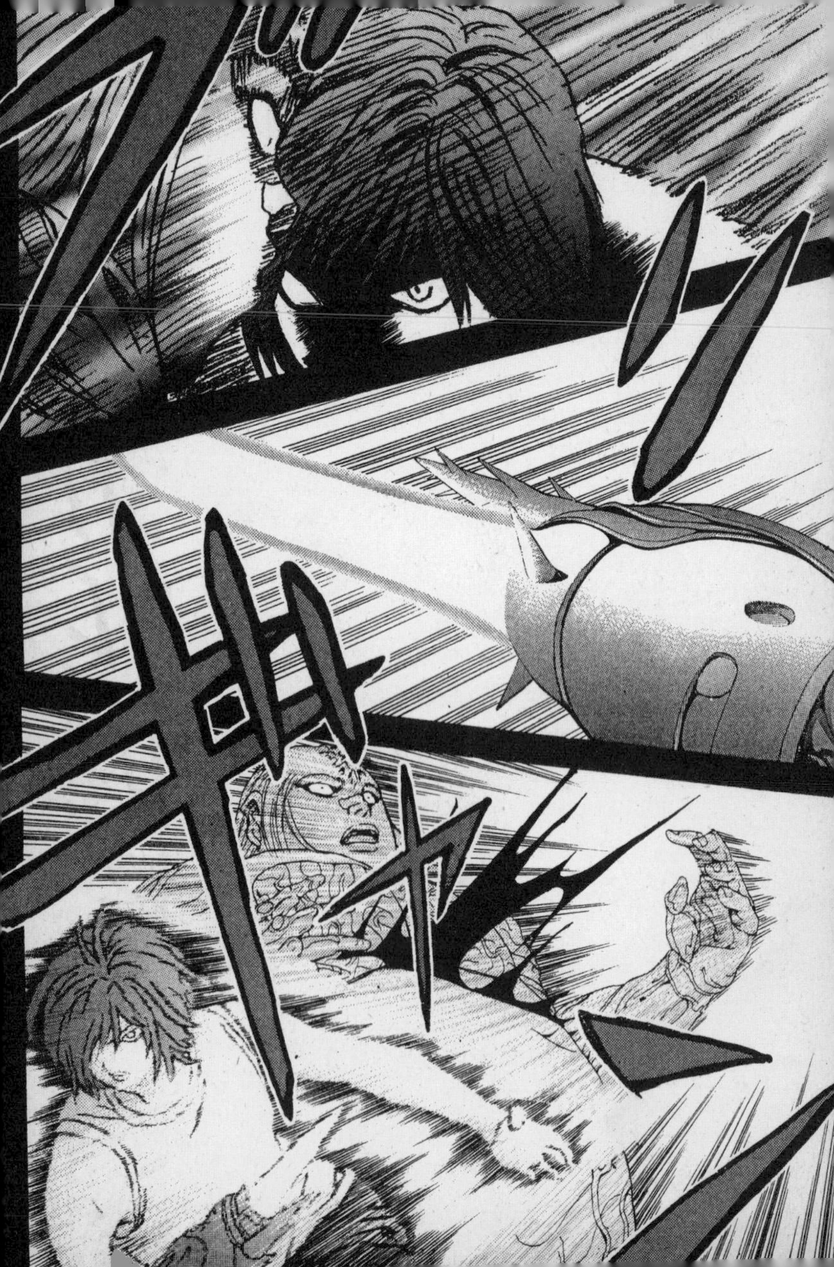

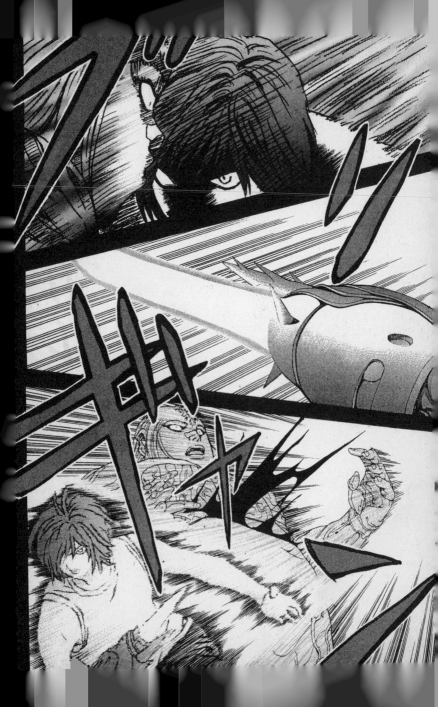

Erp.
HMM...
HE'S FAST!
DID YOU SEE HOW FAST HE MOVED?!
A MINUTE AGO, I THOUGHT HE WAS DONE FOR!
NO SURPRISE. THE CODON STIMULATES ENERGY FORCES ON THE CELLULAR LEVEL.
BUT EVEN SO...
What is this?! My body feels incredibly light...
I feel power surging through my whole body.
And this fire in my right arm.
It's like some demon crawled in and it's taking me over.

Is this...

...me that's suddenly gotten so strong?!
LOOK!
THAT'S AMAZING!
HEH HEH. ♡

FORGETFUL LITTLE MONKEY.
HAS IT NOT YET DAWNED ON YOU THAT AXEL WILL KEEP RISING NO MATTER HOW MANY TIMES HE FALLS?
YOU WON'T STOP HIM WITH ANYTHING AS TRIVIAL AS KILLING HIM.
!?
Rarr!
Hahr!
Ha?!
SO...HOT! THE PLACE WHERE HE CUT ME...IT FEELS LIKE IT'S ON FIRE!
BURNING, MELTING, DISSOLVING...
CAN'T REGENERATE ...!
I THOUGHT THE STRONGER THE MAN THE STRONGER HIS CODON ...
...BUT WITH THIS KID...

SLASH
Yeeoooooohhhh!!
I CAN'T BELIEVE... HE CHARGES ME HEAD ON?!

...MA
TO...
T-TOMA?!
SUCH A SWIFT INCLINATION IN TEMPERATURE... SO MUCH HEAT.
AREN'T YOU CONCERNED?
OUR THRESHOLD'S A LOT HIGHER THAN THEIRS.

AXEL! DON'T BACK DOWN!
HUMAN A-BOMB!
END IT THIS TIME! NOW!
Human A-Bomb!

WHAT ON EARTH...?!

End of EPISODE 7 - Invoking the Codon
To Be Continued in Volume 2!

In the next pulse-pounding volume of *Warriors of Tao*...

Karma deploys two Earth gladiators--the dangerously gorgeous and seductive Locutus and by-the-book hit man Leon--to assassinate Toma! It's a no-holds-barred intergalactic street brawl, and the bloodshed is just beginning!

PROFESSIONAL-WRESTLING-STYLE SPEECHES!

PESTILENT PURSUERS!

HAPLESS HEROES!

WARRIORS OF TAO

VOL. 2

AVAILABLE NOVEMBER 2004!

TOKYOPOP
.remote.™
She can be his eyes,
but can she make him feel...
M
MATURE
AGES 18+
©2003 Seimaru Amagi and Tetsuya Koshiba.
©2004 TOKYOPOP Inc. All Rights Reserved.
www.TOKYOPOP.com

COLLAGE™
BY AHMED HOKE
"[A] MASTERFUL MIX OF MANGA AND HIP-HOP..."
--THE WASHINGTON POST
BOMB
TOKYOPOP®
OT
OLDER TEEN
AGE 16+

# STOP!

## This is the back of the book.
## You wouldn't want to spoil a great ending!

This book is printed "manga-style," in the authentic Japanese right-to-left format. Since none of the artwork has been flipped or altered, readers get to experience the story just as the creator intended. You've been asking for it, so TOKYOPOP® delivered: authentic, hot-off-the-press, and far more fun!

# DIRECTIONS

If this is your first time reading manga-style, here's a quick guide to help you understand how it works.

It's easy... just start in the top right panel and follow the numbers. Have fun, and look for more 100% authentic manga from TOKYOPOP®!

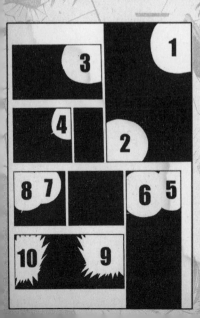